TABLE OF CONTENTS

## FOREWORD

The report on Mergers and Competition Policy, prepared by the OECD Committee of Experts on Restrictive Business Practices, is designed as a follow-up to an earlier report by the Committee on market power and the law, which was published in 1970. The present report pays particular attention to the economic aspects of mergers and their implications for government policy. It analyses the economic effects of mergers with special reference to available empirical evidence, describes the different systems of merger control in existence in Member countries, considers the special problems raised by international mergers and, finally, presents some general conclusions and policy options for Member Governments and suggestions for future action.

The report was approved by the Committee of Experts on Restrictive Business Practices in June, 1974, and generally reflects the position as of that date.

# MERGERS
# AND COMPETITION
# POLICY

**Report of the Committee of Experts
on Restrictive Business Practices**

*The Organisation for Economic Co-operation and Development (OECD) was set up under a Convention signed in Paris on 14th December, 1960, which provides that the OECD shall promote policies designed :*

— *to achieve the highest sustainable economic growth and employment and a rising standard of living in Member countries, while maintaining financial stability, and thus to contribute to the development of the world economy;*

— *to contribute to sound economic expansion in Member as well as non-member countries in the process of economic development;*

— *to contribute to the expansion of world trade on a multilateral, non-discriminatory basis in accordance with international obligations.*

*The Members of OECD are Australia, Austria, Belgium, Canada, Denmark, Finland, France, the Federal Republic of Germany, Greece, Iceland, Ireland, Italy, Japan, Luxembourg, the Netherlands, New Zealand, Norway, Portugal, Spain, Sweden, Switzerland, Turkey, the United Kingdom and the United States.*

\*\*

## Chapter I

## MERGERS, COMPETITION AND ECONOMIC PERFORMANCE

### Definition

1.   A distinction is often made between "merger" and "take over",
where "merger" is used to describe the process of voluntary fusion
between 2 or more companies, and "takeover" usually means the acquisition of control through share purchase without the agreement of the
directors of a company. For the purpose of this study, however, the
term merger will be used to describe both processes. In addition, the
term will be applied to any acquisiton of control, however obtained.

### Introduction

2.   To appreciate the reasons for a concern about mergers it is useful
to have an understanding of the functions of competition and what different countries endeavour to achieve by their policies towards it.
Generally speaking competition policy is one amongst a number of policies which are designed to secure national economic and social goals.
It is thought to make a major contribution to their attainment through
its effects on 3 aspects of market mechanisms. First, competition by
exerting pressure on prices induces firms to produce their outputs in
the most efficient and least cost manner. This pressure on prices also
stimulates firms to anticipate the changing composition of demand by
seeking new products and production processes which widen the range of
consumer choice and reduce unit costs. Firms which are technically efficient and technically progressive are rewarded through the competitive
mechanism, while those which are not are penalised. The third contribution of competition is towards ensuring that there is an efficient
allocation of resources between industries and that output is not either
artificially restricted or produced in greater quantities than are
consistent with the maximum attainable economic welfare. In the absence
of significant barriers to the allocation of resources capital and
labour will move into industries which are earning high profits and
out of those which earn low. Thus, through the more effective meeting
of consumer demands competition ensures that within and between industries resources are allocated to the most efficient firms.

3.    Improved efficiency and resource allocation are not the only contribution. Competition policy, by avoiding an undue concentration of economic power may also contribute materially to the major goals of general economic policy which are usually agreed to be the following :

     i) the attainment of full employment;
    ii) price stability;
  iii) a satisfactory balance of payments;
   iv) a suitable rate of economic growth; and
    v) an efficient distribution of economic resources.

In addition there may be other goals whose attainment competition policy may assist, such as regional employment, environmental control, defence policies, health etc., but it is not usual to consider that these are considerably affected by the intensity and forms of competition. Although it is relevant to note that they might be a concern of competition policy, the relationships will not be developed or considered further in this Chapter.

4.    Not all countries place the same stress on each of these major general economic goals and differences should be expected to arise because of the dynamic nature of market economies. The stress is generally towards improved economic performance and separate aspects of this will be emphasised at different times and stages of economic development. Nevertheless, within the diversity it is possible to see that a major concern exists over the increasing concentration of control of economic resources. This process appears to be taking place in most developed economies and is arising for a number of reasons. Developments in international trade, changes in technology and financial and management techniques and other factors such as tax policies appear to be influencing the growth of large firms relative to small. This leads then to increasing concentration because large firms are growing relatively more quickly both internally and externally by merger. Both kinds of growth raise important questions because of their contribution to high concentration, and these are at the heart of competition policies. Such empirical evidence as there is raises a doubt doubt as to whether the levels of concentration prevailing in some industries in the United States and the United Kingdom are justified by economies of scale in plant and firm operation (1).

5.    High concentration is of major concern because it is one of the key elements of market structure which most influences behaviour and economic performance. It is believed that competition is generally related to the level of concentration of supply in markets, and possibly even over an economy; the higher the levels of concentration

---

1) "Barriers to New Competition" by J.S. Bain, Harvard University Press 1956. "Economies of Scale in Manufacturing Industry" by C.F. Pratten, Cambridge University Press 1971.

the more likely it is that active competition between firms will decline. Indeed the belief is that the most important factor determining the forms and intensity of competition is the fewness or otherwise of the number of sellers. In situations of high concentration the firms in a market will take account of each others prices and product-promotion policies and the potential for implicit or explicit collusion to reduce competitive forces and maximise profits is greatest. This does not mean that such potential will always be realised, but a necessary condition for its existence is the fact of high concentration. As more evidence becomes available it is being increasingly recognised that mergers now make a major contribution to this process.

## History

6.   Historically, the part played by mergers in increasing concentration in the United States, the United Kingdom and Germany has been shown to be important. There have been 3 major merger waves in the United States, 1887-1905, 1916-1929 and post-World War II. The first wave resulted in greatly increased market concentration because of horizontal merger. It is estimated that 15 per cent of all employees and plants in manufacturing industry were involved, and about 3,000 independent firms disappeared, the greater majority being in consolidations of 5 or more firms. The second merger wave resulted in the disappearance of about 12,000 firms, but it differed from the first in that a major component was mergers in the public utility sector and the mergers in manufacturing industry did not result in large increases in market concentration as in the first wave. The 2 periods have been described as "mergers for monopoly" and "mergers for oligopoly". It is suggested that the anti-trust laws may well have discouraged the multi-firm groupings which characterised the first period, and possibly the opportunities for such groupings may have been exhausted. However, the influence of anti-trust appears to have extended into the third wave which commenced after World War II. The data on this wave is more complete than on the others. The Federal Trade Commission recorded 11,668 mergers in manufacturing and mining between 1945 and 1965, and there were an additional 4,933 from 1966 to 1968. An analysis of the size of firm acquired and the markets of acquirer and acquired suggest that, relatively, the acquired firms were considerably smaller than the acquirer, and operated in markets which were distinct; so a substantial proportion were "conglomerate" mergers. The consequence of this change has almost certainly been an increase in the level of overall concentration in the United States economy, although there is some question about the extent to which market concentration has increased. It has been estimated that by 1970 overall concentration measured by the share of total value added held by the largest 100 companies has increased to 33 per cent from 30 per cent in 1954. The marked move towards

conglomerate rather than horizontal or vertical merger is generally accepted to be due to the strict application of anti-trust (1).

7.    The long term trends of market concentration are less well documented for the United Kingdom, but it would appear that there was a major merger wave at approximately the time towards the end of the 19th century as in the United States, and similarly, it was "merger for monopoly", with the predominate type of merger being between 5 or more independent firms. In the inter-war years the pattern was probably different to the United States so there is some support for the suggestion that the "merger for monopoly" motive persisted for much longer. As there was no legislation against such combinations this difference is not surprising. For the post-war period adequate merger statistics were not collected before 1954, but a series is now available from that year up to date. This shows relative stability in the numbers of firms and value of acquisitions until 1959 when both began to increase. Evidence is becoming available which suggests that the widespread dissolution of cartels following the 1956 Restrictive Trade Practices Act caused, with other factors, a major change in the competitive climate and led directly to increased merger activity. A peak was reached in 1965, when there were 1,000 recorded mergers with £ 517 million of assets acquired. By 1971 the assets acquired had increased to £ 911 million while the total number fell to 884. From 1954 to 1965 horizontal mergers predominated, being 67 per cent by number and 71 per cent by value of assets, but since the operation of the 1965 Act which gave power to control certain mergers it would appear that there has been a developing trend towards diversified merger. Of those considered under the Act 9 per cent in 1966 were diversified and this has risen to 24 per cent during the first 9 months of 1972. There was also a rising trend in the value of assets acquired in diversified merger : in 1966 for all mergers over £10 million they were 5 per cent of assets acquired and this rose to 33 per cent in 1972.

8.    Both market and overall concentration has been increasing in the United Kingdom. By 1970 the share of manufacturing net output held by the largest 100 firms had risen to 50 per cent compared with 26 per cent in 1953, and 16 per cent in 1909. It is believed that, at least in the post-War period, the greater part of this increase has been due to increased market concentration. The importance of mergers in the movement has been examined in 2 studies, and these indicate that they have been responsible for about 40 per cent of the increase in market

1) Convenient sources for the evidence on mergers and concentration in the United States of America is given in "Industrial Market Structure and Economic Performance" by F.M. Scherer, and J.M. Blair "Economic Concentration" New York 1972, p. 69.

concentration, so it would follow that they have been similarly important in increasing overall concentration (1).

9.    In Germany mergers must be notified to the Federal Cartel Office
when they meet certain criteria. Thus it is possible to see a continu-
ously rising trend since 1958 with exceptionally high growth rates in
1969 and 1970. In 1958, there were only 15 mergers which met the notification criteria, in 1968, there were 65; 1969 : 168; 1970 : 305;
1971 : 220; 1972 : 269; and 1973 : 242. Looking only at the substantial
mergers, defined by the same method as is applied by the American Federal Trade Commission, the figures are : 1968 : 16; 1969 : 61; 1971 :
69; and 1972 : 75 (2). The German data also show as for the United
States of America and the United Kingdom the increasing popularity of
the conglomerate merger. In 1966 they represented, for substantial
mergers excluding banks and insurance companies, less than 1 per cent
of assets acquired, but by 1972 this had increased quite dramatically
to 31 per cent. By number the change over the period was from 8 to 42
per cent. With regard to overall concentration, the 100 biggest industrial  enterprises increased their share in the total turnover of industry from approximately 34 per cent in 1954 to approximately 50 per
cent in 1969. The 50 biggest enterprises, 0.001 per cent of the total,
now account for 40 per cent of industry turnover. In respect of both
the trend and the degree of concentration, Germany has now out-paced
all the other members of the European Community (3).

High concentration and its adverse consequences

10.    Three adverse consequences are likely to follow from high levels
of concentration. First, a failure to realise the optimum allocation
of resources between industries. This arises where one firm, or a
group of firms acting collusively, can set a price so that it will always exceed the additional cost of supply. Provided the demand curve
were not completely inelastic, consumers would buy more if prices were
lower, i.e. under the conditions of workable competition. Thus profit
maximisation by the firms or colluding group has an output restricting effect from which follows that there will be too few resources in
concentrated industries. The second adverse consequence concerns the
internal efficiency of firms. Control over price and profit from either
dominant firms or collusive behaviour may well reduce the pressure to
the continuous improvement of products and processes which is brought

1) The Effects of Mergers on Concentration : United Kingdom Manufacturing Industry, 1954-65. Journal of Industrial Economics, November
   1971, and forthcoming Hart, Utton and Walshe, Mergers and Economic
   Concentration.

2) Federal Cartel Office Reports, 1969 to 1972.

3) Federal Cartel Office Report 1971 and P. Duesberg in Wirtschaft and
   Wettbewerb 1972.

about by competition. Lack of competition may also result in technical backwardness and a failure to innovate as well as the retention of sub-optimal capacity long beyond the point of economic justification. Third, persistence of higher than average rates of profit may unfavourably affect the distribution of income in society. This may occur in a number of ways. Highly concentrated industries earning high profits may transmit their market power to trade unions with the result that also wages and salaries contain a monopoly profit element. This ability to pay higher wages may also extend to being able to increase prices by more than is sufficient to cover the increased costs, so prices may also be adversely affected. Moreover, high levels of concentration tend to be self-perpetuating and even self-increasing. When prices in an oligopolistic industry are set above the cost of additional supply, new firms may be tempted to enter the industry. However, the dominant firms may be in a position to raise economically unjustified barriers to entry. For example, they may be able to exact discriminatory discounts from their suppliers, thus placing smaller firms at a disadvantage. Or, they may be in a strong position to engage in predatory pricing designed to drive out new entrants. The dominant firms may enjoy similar advantage in branching into new growth products as the industry develops. 300

11.   An additional adverse consequence which may be of some importance concerns the performance of a country in foreign trade. A lack of competitiveness leading to technical backwardness in products and processes may result in a declining export trade and an increasing import trade. This effect is more likely to show itself as the competitive implications of the reductions in tariff and non-tariff barriers are worked out in the future. Insofar as the level of effective demand and employment has to be reduced to help control a declining external balance this aspect of deficient performance may be quite serious at particular times.

12.   The predictions of theory have been subject to empirical testing of two kinds. First, there have been specific industry studies. Amongst the most thorough examples of these have been the investigations by the United Kingdom Monopolies Commission. These were, of course, directed to the questions of structure, behaviour and performance. Examples of each kind of deficient performance have been found; in 8 cases out of 23 persistently high rates of profit were found to be against the public interest in industries which were able to restrict output and deter new entry. Industries with low profit rates and high concentration have also not escaped criticism if the low rate of return was a consequence of a lack of technical progressiveness and the undue retention of high-cost sub-optimal capacity.

10

13.    Exceptions have also been found to the theoretical predictions :
the main supplier of cigarette and tobacco processing machinery was
found not to be acting against the public interest even though its
profit rates were some way above average; the Commission found that
the firm was technically efficient and faced substantial competition.
The manufacturers of flat glass were found not to be operating against
the public interest and the Commission made a point of stressing the
technical progressiveness of the principal firm. However, it should
be stressed that these are exceptions to a general tendency.

14.    In addition to specific investigations cross-section industry
studies have been made of the consequences of high concentration.
These present special problems of interpretation as the predictions
are about performance as a consequence of structure; and concentration,
although often more important and related to other elements, is not
the only aspect to be considered. Nevertheless, the empirical cross-
section investigations of concentration and performance, while not
conclusive beyond all doubt, when taken with the evidence on economies
of scale, do give strong support to the predictions, and therefore support the view that concern needs to be shown about increased concentration.

15.    The investigations of structure/performance which are of most
relevance for the benefits of competition are those which relate concentration to profitability, technical efficiency and innovation. The
interest in profitability is in allocative efficiency. If the firms in
an industry earn above average profits, and these persist through time,
then it may be concluded that market signals (high profits) indicate
that resources should move into the industry but are prevented because
of some substantial entry barriers. There have been numerous tests,
which with one notable exception have concluded that high rates of
profit and high levels of concentration are positively associated with
each other. The exception has since been criticised on the ground that
the method of data preparation biased the results, but an alternative
suggestion is that the profit results may have been affected by open
inflation or price control and this would explain the divergence. However, the result itself is agnostic rather than contrary to the other
findings, so the weight of most of the empirical evidence would therefore agree with the suggested positive relationship (1).

16.    The question of technical efficiency has been investigated less
thoroughly than has profitability, possibly because of the difficulty
in obtaining data, and also perhaps it might be thought, in a very

---

1) A convenient non-technical summary of the evidence on concentration
   and performance is made by L. Weiss in "Frontiers of Quantitative
   Economics", Ch. 9, North Holland 1971.

approximate sense, that technical efficiency would be at least reflected in profit rates. One measure of efficiency is the extent to which firms avail themselves of the economies of scale, so there have been attempts to relate the extent of sub-optimal plant to concentration to see whether there were any systematic relationships. If economies of scale were substantial in relation to size of industry output, then it would be expected that there would be few plants, that these would be of at least minimum efficient size, and as a consequence the proportion of industry output produced in plants smaller than the minimum efficient size would be correspondingly small. Investigation of the concentration/sub-optimal capacity relationship leads to the suggestion that highly concentrated industries do have only a small proportion of output coming from sub-optimal plants, but the picture is less clear with unconcentrated industries where both high and low proportions exist. Where there is a high proportion of output coming from sub-optimal plant it would appear that there are substantial opportunities for the exploitation of economies of scale. On the other hand, if the concept of technical efficiency is widened beyond the size of the plant and is extended to the size of the firm as an attempt to explain existing levels of industry concentration the picture is different. While there may be many opportunities for economies to be realised by building larger plants, the evidence that the efficiency of firms continues to increase as they acquire more and more plants in their own or in other industries is not substantial. Generally speaking, many industries have higher concentration levels than are justified on the grounds of the greater efficiency of larger firms.

17. The final aspect of industry structure and performance which is discussed here is that between concentration and technical progressiveness. It has been suggested, with some measure of truth, that while the loss to society from allocative efficiency is important, if more concentrated industries produce higher rates of growth then this can in principle more than compensate for the welfare losses of monopoly and oligopoly. Although growth is determined by many factors, the crucial importance of technical progressiveness is generally acknowledged. It seems reasonable, therefore to look for links between structure and technical progress, particularly when frequent claims are made about the critical role of large firms. Direct analysis of concentration and growth has produced contradictory results so the main investigations have been indirect. It has been assumed that either the amount of money spent on research and development or the number of patents obtained are satisfactory indices of "innovation" (innovation is assumed to be closely related to technical progress). These are not perfect indicators but this has not prevented useful work being done in 2 directions. First, on the question of whether large firms are better than small firms at making technical innovations and introducing

12

them into commercial practice. Studies for the United States and the
United Kingdom have produced the same broad conclusion, that once a
threshold of firm size is reached, which is relatively small in both
countries, increasing size does not add proportionately more to R & D
activity or success. Moreover, size of firm is not a necessary condition, there are sufficient examples to show conclusively that significant innovations are made and brought to commercial success by small
firms.

18.    On the direct relationship between R & D and concentration positive results have emerged, but when account is taken of the opportunity
for technological innovation, increased concentration has only a small
positive effect. The conclusion appears to be that some degree of concentration can be beneficial but high levels of concentration very
rarely have a favourable effect. As high concentration can restrict
entry and hence the number of independent sources of innovation activity it will only be in very exceptional cases that it would be conducive to innovation. This conclusion is further weakened when account
is taken of Government involvement in R & D for there is no reason why
small and medium-sized firms cannot benefit to the same extent from
these programmes as large firms.

19.    This brief review of the evidence of the effects of concentration
on performance indicates that the results have implications for mergers
policy. Where mergers produce high concentration then it would appear
that there is a high probability of one or more of these detrimental
effects arising as a consequence. To balance this there is the possibility that mergers between small or medium-sized firms which do not
result in high concentration, may make it possible for them to achieve
economies and thus promote competition. Thus the effect of any parti- *Concl*
cular merger will depend upon the relevant market situation, which
will include the relative sizes of competing firms and the extent of
international trade in the product. More generally in economies where
the private ownership of capital predominates, takeover and merger may
perform two further useful economic functions by transferring resources
from less to more efficient uses and by providing a stimulus to firms
to improve their efficiency through the threat of takeover. If this
happens, then these would be favourable effects to set against the unfavourable consequences of increased concentration. That these effects
do occur cannot be doubted, but their importance has not yet been adequately assessed. It is, however, possible to make a limited examination of the efficiency of the operation of the transfer of resources
effect by looking at the evidence of the "private" benefit from mergers. The private benefit would be measured by the subsequent performance of the merged firm, and would not include wider social costs and
benefits.

20.    Two kinds of evidence are available on the "private" effects of mergers, that derived from interviews with the executives of merged firms, and that derived from statistical  analyses of such data as growth of sales, profitability, or share price. The evidence of interviews is,  of necessity,  derived from small samples and hence needs to be interpreted with care, and possibly with additional background statistical information. There have been two recent such studies, one for the United States and the other for the United Kingdom (1). While not being identical in all respects they were both concerned with the success of mergers. In the United States study the executives concerned thought that 19 out of their 69 (20 per cent) mergers were unsuccessful. Interestingly enough the highest failure rates occur amongst conglomerate mergers. For the United Kingdom in a sample of 38 mergers the executives thought in 17 (45 per cent) cases that there had been no economic or other benefits within a two year period, and when asked about additional benefits (over the initial two years) 21 (55 per cent) thought that there would be none in 5 years.

21.    These are, of course, very crude indicators based on impression, no doubt well informed, but nevertheless on very small samples. The statistical approach is able to get over this problem to some extent but has its own weaknesses. Nevertheless, a recent United States study of 478 firms from Fortune's list of 500 largest industrial corporations for 1951 has produced some interesting results on the private benefits to shareholders from merger activity (2). Reid compared increases in sales for firms with different degrees of merger intensity and related these to the percentage increase in the price of common stock and the percentage increase in return to the stockholders for the period 1951-61. He found that while firms which grew mainly internally did poorly in terms of sales growth they did better than the merger-prone groups in terms of return to stockholders. Thus, this evidence does not strongly suggest that merger is especially effective in producing private benefit. It is, of course, possible that the merger-prone firms sacrificed profitability over that period to achieve growth as a means of increasing long-term profitability, but the data would not resolve this particular question. In addition, short-term profit rates are not the only measure of private benefits, perhaps not even the most important. Managements may value lower more stable returns than higher but unstable, and while it is difficult to measure the effects of mergers on profit rates over long periods, stability of return may lead to economic gains.

---

1) J. Kipling "Why Mergers Miscarry", Harvard Business Review 1967, and G. Newbould "Management and Merger Activity".
2) S.R. Reid, Mergers, Management and the Economy, McGraw Hill, 1968.

22.    The most thorough and up-to-date study in the United Kingdom (1)
has been concerned with the performance of firms before and after merger and with the efficiency of the stock market as a means of enabl-
ing resources to move into more profitable uses. Singh's results show
that, on average, 60-65 per cent of firms which were taken over had
profitability, growth and valuation ratios which were lower than their
industry average, so broadly speaking firms which performed "better"
took over firms which performed "worse" (in private benefit terms).
The success of merger is, however, in question, as 57 per cent of merged firms in the sample had a post-acquisition profit record which was
worse than the record of the separate firms before merger. This figure
of relative failure in terms of private profitability is broadly similar to that found in the interview studies. Singh also found, that
while firms with higher profitability took over firms with lower, the
ability to resist takeover seemed to be related to size. The large and
medium-sized firms had a much lower probability of being acquired than
had small firms, and Singh concluded from this that it was possible
for a firm to defeat takeover bids by acquiring other firms itself.

23.    These results have some significance for the efficient operation
of the Stock Exchange. It is thought that the latter performs two useful economic functions : it assesses and prices the management efficiency of firms, and it allocates capital to those which promise the
highest rewards. Some part of this process is seen in merger situations, and if there is a general tendency for more efficient firms to
acquire the less efficient through takeover bids then improved resource
allocation may be achieved directly in this way. It may also be secured
if the potential threat of takeover spurs other inefficient managements
to improve their performance. If however, inefficient firms are able to
to resist takeover by becoming acquiring firms themselves and if there
is only a weak tendency for efficiency to be improved after merger then
the functions of Stock Exchanges in facilitating mergers may be called
into question.

Conclusions on performance

24.    This review has put forward the economic analysis and some of
the empirical testing has been applied to mergers and their effect on
concentration and performance. The argument has been advanced that
mergers contribute in a significant manner to increased concentration
and this is generally supported by the data for the United States,
the United Kingdom and Germany. A review was then made of concentration and the evidence of the private, as distinct from the social,
benefit from mergers. Four measures of performance have been used :

───────────────────

1) A. Singh "Takeover" Cambridge University Press, 1971.

industry profit rates, technical efficiency in the sense of the extent of sub-optimal plant, technical progressiveness, through the proxy variable of research and development expenditures, and the private profits of firms before and after merger. The conclusion which emerges can at present only be tentative; it is that the suggestion that increased concentration beyond certain points results in allocative inefficiency is probably justified; the technical efficiency question has not yet been resolved and while there is some evidence that increased concentration may not result in the preservation of sub-optimal capacity many industries are more highly concentrated than efficiency requires; and that marginally, increased concentration below high levels may be conducive to technical progressiveness, but its effect is not strong. Although it cannot be said that sufficient evidence has been accumulated to lead to a general presumption about the success or otherwise of mergers, it does not appear that most have achieved the expectations of the acquiring companies in terms of increased profitability. This must inevitably raise the question of the social gain and whether it has been enhanced or reduced. It also raises the question of the efficiency of stock markets in assisting the beneficial resource allocation effects which are potentially available in some mergers.

25. While each of the pieces of evidence quoted above are probably insufficient when considered singly, when put together they strongly support the case that the social costs which may arise from mergers are by no means automatically offset by even the private gains. The case for merger, therefore, cannot be wholeheartedly supported on economic grounds, nor can it be readily assumed that, left to itself, the market is an efficient method of forcing firms towards increased efficiency and profitability. This does not necessarily lead to the conclusion that all mergers should be prohibited, or that there be direct Government intervention to make the market work efficiently. Two approaches to policy over mergers have emerged as a consequence of this overall conclusion. The first is to attempt to make a calculation of the balance of benefit from the prospective increase in efficiency or competitive strength of merged companies weighed against the possible detriment arising from the increase in market power as a consequence of larger size. This would take account of circumstances where a merger led to an enhancement of competition compared with the previously existing situation. This calls for a case-by-case approach and will try to assess all the consequences for structure, behaviour and performance. The other approach concentrates on the structural effects of the merger, the argument being that increased concentration leads inevitably to some detriment as a consequence of decreased competition and the fact that there may be increased efficiency will not automatically mean that this will accrue to consumers due to the lack of

competitive pressure. Mergers are therefore judged in terms of their underlined effects on the structure of industries and the consequences for the competitive mechanism. *whether to investigate mergers or not.*

26.    Neither of these approaches implies that every merger which takes place could or should be examined. Investigation is, itself, a real cost to society and many small mergers which bring minute efficiency gains or losses will not justify such an expenditure of resources. Some small mergers may even promote competition and not reduce it. At which sizes and what circumstances mergers are subject to possible control depends upon factors specific to each national economy. The existing levels of concentration, the size distribution of firms, the extent of foreign trade, the growth of technology and overall growth of the economy as well as any social objectives will be the main deciding factors.

## Motives for merger

27.    In the preceding section it was suggested that merger and the stock market are not very efficient mechanisms for transferring resources to more profitable uses and improving profitability after a merger. This, in part, is due to the range of motives in mergers, not all of which are concerned with efficiency or perhaps increased private profitability. Some mention of the different motives for merger is useful because they have different implications for public policy. Twelve main motives are suggested as being the most frequent :

    1. To increase market power.
    2. To build an empire.
    3. To gain the promotional profits.
    4. To expand production without price reduction.
    5. To acquire capacity at reduced prices.
    6. To obtain real economies of scale.
    7. To obtain pecuniary economies of scale.
    8. To rationalise production.
    9. To use complementary resources.
    10. To spread risks by diversification.
    11. The failing firm argument.
    12. To merge because of tax advantages.

There is no substantial body of research which suggests the relative importance of these motives. It is possible that several will be present in most mergers, and as the balance of private and social cost and benefit may be different for each it is impossible to decide without further analysis what is the overall gain to society from a proposed merger. This mixture of private and social benefits and costs confirms the earlier analysis that there can be no overriding presumption in favour or against all mergers.

*Analysis*

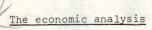

## The economic analysis

28.　　The main thread of the discussion of mergers in this chapter has been that they have consequences for the structure, behaviour and performance of the industries in which they take place. The review of the empirical evidence has shown some of these and it is now the purpose of this section to set out the main framework of the economic analysis of an individual merger so the aspects which are most relevant to public policies may be identified. This analysis, of course, is only of relevance for those mergers which may have significant economic effects.

29.　　As the merger of two or more firms by definition increases concentration, a distinction must be made between those which increase industrial and overall concentration and those which only increase overall concentration. Conglomerate mergers are of the latter type and horizontal and some vertical are the former. The main analysis of this section is directed towards horizontal and vertical mergers, and conglomerate mergers will be discussed separately.

30.　　The starting point is the possible consequences for the structure of the industry in which the merger takes place. Two main aspects have been identified as being most important for their effects on competition : the degree of concentration and barriers to entry. The immediate effect of a merger is to increase the degree of concentration because it changes the number and size distribution of firms, and this by itself may have detrimental consequences if it allows the merged firms to raise prices through the exercice of market power. There may, however, be other consequences which change the degree of concentration. If economies of scale are potentially available to two firms then it is possible that they are also available to other pairs of firms, so there may be a general tendency towards merger and some of these, by improving efficiency, may promote competition. On the other hand firms may also wish to take advantage of the market power aspects of joining together, or mergers may take place as a defensive reaction to an earlier regrouping. In these circumstances one change in concentration sets in motion a series of others, and if, as is suggested above, these may come about because of the potential market power advantages the short and long term consequences for competition are likely to be detrimental.

31.　　Barriers to entry are the second aspect of structure which may be affected. If there are economies of scale which can be realised through merger then it is possible that these may act as a deterrent if merged firms thereby achieve some major cost advantage over potential entrants. This is likely to be the case where new entrants may only enter at low levels of output which impose a substantial cost disadvantage on them. While there are cases where the economies of scale are so substantial and have these consequences, possibly the more common situation is that where the "economies" only arise as a consequence of the enhanced market power of the larger firm. These constitute an artificial barrier to entry. Additional artificial barriers may be raised or strengthened if the merger results in a strengthening of product differentiation through legal rights in designs, patents, know-how and other means conferring protection from competition by other products or manufacturing processes. 300

32.   Increased product differentiation is also an aspect of behaviour which may change as a consequence of merger. The larger firm may have the resources to engage in substantial non-price forms of competition of which advertising is a major kind. While some form of differentiation may result in a real widening of consumer choice it can be questioned whether any important economic benefits are conferred on consumers by the greater part of non-price competition which is a feature of oligopoly.

33.   Other forms of behaviour may also be affected. The larger firm may be able to engage in discriminatory pricing amongst customers if raised barriers to entry enable it to fragment sectors of the market, and it may also be able to practise predatory pricing of some kind against existing competitors. The extent to which these two kinds of behaviour may be practised depends upon the existing legal constraints in different countries and upon the possibility of maintaining the short-term gains which they bring. These can only be turned into long-term gains if it is possible to raise entry barriers so high that when firms are driven out they and others cannot enter. Such situations are comparatively rare, so the most common forms of price behaviour which are likely to emerge or be strngthened are price leadership and parallel pricing. Where this does occur the market power benefits accrue to the other firms in the industry as well as the merged firms.

34.   The analysis of the potential structural and behavioural consequences have concentrated on those aspects of mergers which are likely to enhance market power, but the consequences for the performance of the firms and the industry have also to be taken into account. Probably the most commonly stated motive for merger is to improve efficiency, and if this is the result then there is at least the potential for the efficiency gains being used through enhanced competition to offset the market power consequences. In the context of an individual case efficiency should be defined both in terms of the technical efficiency of production, sales, management and technical progressiveness. In the short term merged firms should be able either to produce the same output with a lower expenditure of real resources, or a greater output with the same resources. In the long term the dynamic effects of improved efficiency might be expected to be apparent through improved products and processes.

Main reason 4 merge

35.    Particular care is required in applying the foregoing principles to vertical mergers. Horizontal integration is a rather indirect route to achieve technical economies of large scale and may lead to increases in market power. Vertical integration, too, may bring about an improved allocation of resources as well as undesirable effects. The optimum degree of vertical integration of any particular industry is also not given once and for all, but varies as technology and the extent of the market change. At any given moment of time, the optimum number of stages of production carried out within a firm will be determined by the condition that, at the margin, no additional transaction can be arranged more cheaply internally than through the market. In addition, vertical integration can lead to a better allocation of firm resources when the market is not perfectly competititve and the firm has to buy its imports at monopolistic prices from lower stage producers. Real gains can therefore be achieved by the vertically integrated enterprise.   However, these gains must be weighed  against adverse effects of the merger. For example, a vertically integrated firm which has monopoly power in one stage may increase barriers to entry through vertical integration. It may also be in a better position to discriminate between different purchasers by monopolisation of raw material supplies or distributive outlets.

36.    Two further considerations arise of a wider kind than the immediate market power and efficiency consequences of a proposed merger. The first concerns the net economic benefit to the community of the internal growth of firms compared with external growth. Because internal growth, either in the same or into another industry is frequently based on some differential efficiency and because it often also promotes competition then it is probably to be preferred, even though in some circumstances it might result in high concentration. Generally, however, the forces which favour internal growth will also favour growth of the small and medium sized firms and there may well be an overall tendency to deconcentration. External growth, on the other hand, will often bring about an immediate increase in market power with potentially reduced competition and no certainty that efficiency will improve sufficiently to restore the balance. This leads to the conclusion that generally, where firms could grow internally they should be encouraged to do so, but the speed with which the improved efficiency is attained compared with merger may be important. If merger secures the efficiency gain more quickly than internal growth for the same increase in market power then it might be preferred.

37.    The second consideration is how the gains from merger are distributed.   Generally speaking competition policies are not major instruments for affecting the distribution of income in society, but occasionally there may be large mergers which do raise such questions

as between producers and consumers and as between one group of workers
and another where the market power of firms is transmitted to the trade
unions of their workers. As between producers and consumers it should
be recognised that competition is the most efficient mechanism for
transferring the gains to consumers and society at large. As between
groups of workers other instruments may be needed.

## The conglomerate merger

38.   The analysis outlined above is applicable to horizontal and vertical mergers where the public policy issue is either the trade-off
between increased efficiency and increased market power or the examination of the effects on structure and behaviour. As such it fits into
the traditional core of economic analysis and, relatively speaking
presents no overwhelming problems. The rapid rise of what is known as
the conglomerate merger has, however, raised new issues, and it must
be acknowledged that they have not yet been satisfactorily solved.
This does not mean that such mergers are outside the sphere of public
policy, it simply means that judgement and care has to be used in making predictions from the general body of economic theory and empirical
research.

39.   A convenient definition of a conglomerate merger is "mergers between companies that do not produce similar products and where neither
is an actual or potential supplier of the other". Customary usage in
the United States and Germany also distinguishes between product extension, market extension and pure conglomerate mergers. The evidence of
the popularity of this type of company growth was given earlier in the
chapter and it need only be noted here that the development has been
startling. It has been claimed that the strict application of the
Celler-Kefauver Act against horizontal mergers in the United States of
America has led to this development, and while the evidence is not in
disagreement there has been no such bias in Germany and the United
Kingdom to account for the changed trend. It is possible that other
constraints on growth in existing markets have become more important
in these 2 countries so they are reflecting a natural tendency towards
greater diversification. If this is so the patterns for mergers for
over developed countries are likely to show similar trends.

40.   The economic consequences of conglomerate mergers have already
been mentioned by the OECD Study "Market Power and Law" (1). In citing
Edwards (2) it is said that "ever-increasing diversification of many

---

1) OECD Market Power and the Law, Paris, 1970.

2) Corwin D. Edwards, The Changing Dimensions of Business Power, St.
   John's Law Review Vol. 44 (1970); see also Economic Report on Cor-
   porate Mergers, Staff Report to the Federal Trade Commission, 1969
   (Part 8A of the Hearings on Economic Concentration before the Sub-
   Committee on Anti-trust and Monopoly, United States Senate).

modern enterprises is changing traditional patterns of business decision  and competitive interaction, especially where large diversified
firms with many products compete with specialised single-product firms'.
Diversified firms, as Edwards states, have the ability "to rechannel
funds and spread risks, subsidise one activity from the proceeds of
another, enjoy the benefits of joint revenue, spread large lump-sum
costs over multiple products, undertake vertical integration, get
bargaining advantages from threats to do so, and resort to reciprocity". This gives them an advantage over their specialist competitors,
thereby changing the traditional pattern of competition. Where they
compete with similarly diversified firms, competition with them is
likely to move away from price competition to non-price forms (e.g.
sales promotion, innovation) due to availability of large financial
funds to retaliate against competitive price cuts. Size and financial
power of firms, factors to which the traditional concept of market
power pays no attention, become thus of primary significance.

41.    The framework for the analysis of the individual conglomerate
merger might be conveniently arranged around the two benefits which
are said to derive from the conglomerate type of structure :
   a) the acquired firm gets access to the existing productive
      resources of the conglomerate and this may improve its tech-
      nical efficiency; and
   b) it gets access to the greater financial strength of the parent
      and this results in such benefits as better credit terms,
      higher discounts, lower input prices etc. However, these may
      provide a financial basis from which to expand by acquiring
      potential competitors, and they may also permit the practice
      of reciprocal dealing.
It should be noted that these have been divided into what might be term-
ed real economies and pecuniary economies and these mean the same
things as for the analysis of horizontal and vertical mergers. The former may raise both efficiency and market power while the latter only
exist as a consequence of the market power of the parent. The questions raised are the same as for horizontal and vertical mergers, how
will the structure of industries be changed, in what ways might behaviour be affected and what are the consequences for performance ? These
are relevant for both the acquiring and acquired firm, but generally
the concern is over the latter and its industry rather than the former, because usually the merger opens new possibilities.

42.    The immediate impact of a conglomerate merger is to leave existing levels of market concentration unchanged, but the entry of a large
diversified firm may set off a defensive reaction amongst other suppliers which leads to mergers amongst them and thereby to increased
concentration. Another main possible influence is the effect on barriers to entry. As there are very few conglomerate mergers, and most

diversification is based on some area of specialisation of the acquiring firm it is possible that these may raise barriers to entry. For
example common areas of technology which have legal protection might
be an important cause of the merger, or the additional real and pecuniary efficiency gains might be a cost barrier to intending entrants.

43.    The possibility of introducing or increasing product differentiation was mentioned earlier as an important element of both structure
and behaviour which might be changed by merger and this may be a particularly important consequence of  the access to the greater financial
resources of the acquiring firm. Other aspects of behaviour may be
affected and, of course, it is in this area that the principal case
against conglomerates is put. The greater financial strength is claimed
to enable the acquirer to practice discriminatory and predatory pricing
and also to be able to move financial resources from market to market.
However, it should be noted that there can be no long-term gain from
these forms of behaviour unless the conglomerate is able to drive out
competitors and heighten entry barriers so that they are unable to
return.

44.    One benefit claimed for conglomerates is that they can make small
mergers and then use their superior efficiency to grow. If this is true
then it is likely that such growth will result in an increased degree
of competition and this would be a considerable economic benefit.
The performance of a conglomerate is therefore of considerable importance in assessing the likely consequences for competition from a
merger. If there are real efficiency gains which may be achieved, and
if there is an efficient mechanism for passing these to consumers in
the form of reduced prices and/or improved products then such mergers
may be of economic benefit. If there are not likely to be efficiency
gains then it is difficult to see what benefits such mergers will
bring. There is, however, the possibility that  in particular cases
increased size could result in decreased efficiency so this must be
taken account of in the analysis. It has been suggested that where
acquisition is made by the exchange of shares there is the possibility
that overall efficiency could decline while the return to shareholders
as earnings per share could increase. It would be important to establish whether this was part of the history of a particular conglomerate
firm, and, even if it was not, whether there were any special factors
in a proposed merger situation which would be likely to produce dis-
economies of size.

45.    Although the economic power of conglomerates may exist only as a
consequence of market power in individual markets, measurement of that
power by traditional economic standards, and proof of its existence,
may be difficult by conventional means. As conglomerate firms compete
in an increasing number of individual markets, the probability that a

merger of two conglomerate firms will produce anti-competitive effects in some markets increases. In analysing such mergers, the evidence relating to each market must first be weighed separately to determine the probability of an anti-competitive effect in such market. Second, all these probabilities must then be considered together to determine if it is more likely than not that an anti-competitive effect will occur in some market.

46. The conglomerate merger movement has not yet been subjected to the same economic analysis as have horizontal and vertical mergers; therefore the predictions of theory about the possible consequences must be interpreted and applied with care in each case since a particular conglomerate merger may be pro- or anti-competitive. However, some generalisations appear possible. For example, the acquisition by a very large firm of a leading firm in a concentrated industry is likely to have anti-competitive effects, including that of entrenching the acquired firm in its leading position. On the other hand, pro-competitive effects are likely to occur when a large conglomerate makes a "foothold" acquisition of a small firm in a concentrated industry; the resources of the conglomerate are available to build the acquired company into a more substantial competitor, thereby perhaps ultimately reducing concentration.

47. As the size of conglomerate mergers increases, so also does the likelihood that the merger will have anti-competitive effects, such as increasing the opportunity for reciprocal dealing and the elimination of potential competition. Size can also present adverse political and social consequences. While a few very large firms may be necessary in some industries for reasons of international competition or high risk or high capital requirements and significant scale economies, an economy dominated by large firms may find that the market structure and performance which result from them may make the normal macro-economic policies either inoperative or very much more costly to implement. The penalty of neglect of the question of market structure then becomes political and social as well as economic. However, no measurable or meaningful analysis of these political and social consequences is yet possible, and the desirability of any particular conglomerate merger must, therefore, continue to be measured by economic analysis.

Overall conclusion

48. It has been argued in this chapter that because mergers contribute to increased concentration, and increased concentration may lead to deficient economic performance some supervision of mergers may be necessary. The evidence of the contribution to social benefits from mergers is not greater and nor does the evidence of private benefit suggest that merger is in all cases the most efficient way of trans-

ferring resources from less to more profitable uses. This is not to
suggest that merger should be replaced by some other transfer mechanism
imposed by governments or private business forces outside the market.
The most efficient, and most beneficial in social benefit terms, and
in all probability, private terms as well, is the competitive mechanism. The maintenance of competition in modern economies which are
becoming increasingly integrated through world trade presents special
problems, and often powerful forces argue for increased market power
because of the international nature of competition. The evidence suggests that such power does not always bring the benefits of the increased efficiency which is necessary for fruitful participation in world
trade. Competition and efficiency are interdependent, to encourage
competition is to encourage economic efficiency and vice versa. The
influence of market structures in this process is decisive, and a
policy about mergers designed to encourage efficiency and reduce undue
market power must play its own part.

Chapter II

## THE OPERATION OF SYSTEMS OF MERGER CONTROL

49.    Action against mergers in the context of competition policy has
so far only been taken in Canada, Germany, the United States, Japan
and the United Kingdom. In a number of other Member countries the
legislation on restrictive business practices contains some provisions
applicable to mergers, for example registration of certain operations
mainly in order to collect more information on mergers, but these
latter provisions do not constitute a comprehensive system of merger
control. The countries involved here are Austria, Belgium, Spain and
Sweden. In addition, a bill including provisions for the control of
mergers within the context of competition laws has been introduced in
Australia, whilst in Ireland and the Netherlands mergers legislation
is currently under consideration. In addition, the Commission of the
European Communities has submitted a proposed regulation for the control of mergers to the Council.

## I. PROVISIONS RELATING TO MERGERS WHICH DO NOT INVOLVE
SPECIFIC CONTROL

50.    In Austria, the present Cartel Act provides, in section 50, that
all mergers - with the exception of those which are of minor economic
interest, i.e accounting for less than 5 per cent of the market - must
be notified for entry in the cartel register. Only those mergers which
have a dominant position on the market are subject to control of abuse,
regardless of whether or not their dominant market position has been
entered in the cartel register. An enterprise  is deemed  market dominating within  the  meaning  of (a) if it faces no or insignificant competition on the market for a particular product or service or (b) if it
accounts for more than 5 per cent of the domestic market and (i) if the domestic market is supplied by two or three enterprises only, or (ii) is
one of the four largest enterprises which together have a total share of
the domestic market of no less than 80 per cent.

51.    In Belgium, the Act on Protection against the Abuse of Economic
Power provides that if a firm found guilty of an abuse commits a further abuse, it may be prohibited by Royal Decree from merging with
another firm. Such a measure has never been applied.

52.    In _Spain_, mergers must be entered in the Final Restrictive Business Practices Register within one month from the conclusion of the
merger agreement if the new enterprise controls 30 per cent or more
of the market or if one of the  parties to the merger already controls
this share of the national market. The object of registration is to
keep the authorities informed of the most important concentrations.
Mergers are not subject to legal restrictions, whatever the size,
nature or importance of the firms involved.

53.    In _Sweden_, the antitrust law does not contain special provisions
on mergers. All mergers are, however, registered by the National Price
and Cartel Office. This register is public. The antitrust authorities
can request any information from the merging firms concerning the
impact on competition from the merger. Merger or consolidation fall
within the scope of the general rule of the Act. When after a legal
procedure a restriction of this kind is found to have harmful effects
by the Market Court, legal negotiation proceedings take place to eliminate the harmful effects.


## II. SYSTEMS INVOLVING SPECIFIC CONTROL OF MERGERS

54.    Administrative or judicial control of mergers has been established in Canada, Germany, the United States, Japan, the United Kingdom,
and the European Communities.

55.    In _Canada_, Section 33 of the Combines Investigation Act provides
that every person who is a party or privy to or knowingly assists in,
or in the formation of a merger as defined in section 2 of the Statute
is guilty of an indictable offence and is liable to imprisonment for
two years. Section 2 gives a very narrow definition of an illegal
merger : it is required that as a result of the merger competition is,
or is likely to be, lessened to the detriment or against the interest
of the public, whether consumers, producers or others. Up to the present time, the courts have given judgement in five merger cases (1) and
they have interpreted the statutory criteria very restrictively.
It seems that the criminal nature of the merger provisions is an ob-
stacle to their application.

56.    Since 1960, however, a "programme of compliance" has been in
operation in Canada under which businessmen are encouraged to discuss

--------------------------------------------------------

1) Four of these cases are analysed in detail in the report "Market
   Power and the Law", OECD, 1970. The fifth being the New Brunswick
   Newspaper case - Regina v. K.C. Irving Ltd. et al in which convic-
   tion on two monopoly and two merger counts was handed down on 24th
   January, 1974, and, in which the companies have indicated their
   intention to appeal the matter. There has, in addition, been one
   case where the defendant pleaded guilty /Regina v. Electric Reduction Company of Canada Ltd. (1970)61 C.P.R. 235/.

their merger proposals with the Director of Investigation and Research before adopting policies which might offend against the law. Business-men are not bound to comply with the Director's opinion, nor is the Director bound by his opinion. To ensure the efficient working of the programme the Director has set out a list of criteria by which the Branch responsible could assess whether a particular merger infringes the law by lessening competition to the detriment or against the inte-rest of the public (1).

57.    In Germany, Section 23 (1) of the Act Against Restraints of Competition requires that all mergers must be reported to the Federal Cartel Office, if (i) the merging firms obtain or increase a share of at least 20 per cent of the relevant market or one of the merging firms has a market share of at least 20 per cent on any other market, or (ii) if the merging firms employed 10,000 or more persons or had sales proceeds of D.M. 500 million or more at any time during the year preceding the merger. This wording makes clear that all types of mer-gers, whether horizontal, vertical or conglomerate, have to be reported, if they fulfil the above requirements. The Federal Cartel Office may request from each participating enterprise information on its market share and sales of a specific kind of goods or commercial services made in the course of the twelve months preceding the merger. If the merger involves at least two enterprises with sales proceeds of D.M. 1 billion or more each during the year preceding the intended merger, advance notification is required, and the merger may only be consum-mated if the Federal Cartel Office does not state within a period of one month that it is examining the merger proposal and if a decree prohibiting the merger has not been issued within a period of four months after notification. Other mergers may voluntarily be submitted for advance clearance and in this case the same time limits apply. In cases of ex post control the time limit is one year from the date of submission of a complete notification.

58.    Section 24 (1) of the Act provides that the cartel authority may prohibit a merger, if it is to be expected that the merger creates or strengthens a market dominating position, unless the participating enterprises prove that the merger also brings about an improvement of the competitive conditions which outweigh the disadvantages of market dominance. An enterprise is market dominating when it has no competi-tors or when it is not exposed to any substantial competition or when it has an overriding market position in relation to its competitors. For this purpose, besides its market share, in particular its financial strength, its access to the supply or sales markets of goods and ser-vices, its links with other enterprises as well as legal or actual

1) D.H.W. Henry, "Mergers in Canada under the Combines Investigation Act" (Texas International Law Forum, Spring 1969, page 5).

barriers to market entry of other enterprises have to be taken into account. It is presumed that an enterprise is market dominating if it has a market share of at least one-third in regard to a certain type of goods or commercial services ; this presumption does not apply when the enterprise recorded a turnover of less than D.M. 250 million in the last complete financial year. Two or more enterprises are deemed market dominating insofar as no substantial competition exists between them and they jointly meet the above mentioned requirements. They are presumed market dominating if three or less enterprises have a combined market share of 50 per cent or more, or five or less enterprises have a combined market share of two-thirds or more; this presumption does not apply to enterprises which recorded a turnover of less than D.M. 100 million in the last complete financial year.

59.   If a merger has been prohibited by the Federal Cartel Office the parties may ask the Minister for Economic Affairs for a special exemption. Such an exemption may only be granted for predominant reasons relating to the economy as a whole and the public interest. In deciding upon the exemption the Minister must also take into consideration the parties' ability to compete on foreign markets /Section 24 (3)7. The entire control system by the Federal Cartel Office and the Minister does, however, not apply, if :

a) the participating enterprises had combined sales proceeds of less than D.M. 500 million during the last business year; or

b) an enterprise with sales proceeds of less than D.M. 50 million during the last business year merges with another enterprise on its own initiative; or

c) the restriction of competition is not expected to take effect in the entire territory in which the Act applies or a substantial part thereof; or

d) a market for goods or commercial services is affected on which there have been sales of less than D.M. 10 million during the last year.

60.   In the United States, the mergers law has developed to a large extent from cases decided in the courts. The amended Section 7 of the Clayton Act, the Celler-Kefauver Act, enacted in 1950 (1), is the principal

---

1) Section 1 of the Clayton Act also applies to mergers. See United States v. First National Bank and Trust Co., 376 U.S. 665 (1964). In addition Section 2 of the Sherman Act may also be applied to mergers when they are aimed at monopolizing any part of trade or commerce within the United States. In addition, the Federal Trade Commission is concerned with mergers. Any company whose assets exceed $250 million must notify the Federal Trade Commission if it intends to acquire another company whose assets exceed $10 million. Similarly, the Federal Trade Commission must be notified of any merger resulting in the formation of a company whose assets exceed $250 million.

statutory basis of merger control and the Supreme Court has interpreted its somewhat general provisions in a number of decisions. The Department of Justice in an effort to aid businessmen in interpreting the law has indicated in its Merger Guidelines the circumstances under which it will generally bring merger cases.

61.    The Celler-Kefauver Act amending Section 7 of the Clayton Act came into operation in 1950. It provides that "no corporation shall acquire the whole or any part of the stock or other share capital or the whole or any part of the assets of another corporation, where the effect of such acquisition may be substantially to lessen competition, or to tend to create a monopoly". Section 7 of the Clayton Act applies not only to mergers between effective competitors (horizontal mergers) but also to vertical and conglomerate mergers which may lessen competition.

62.    With regard to horizontal mergers, the Supreme Court, in the first case decided under Section 7 of the Clayton Act (1), undertook a detailed economic analysis, placing special emphasis on the market shares held by the parties to the merger. In a subsequent decision (2), the Supreme Court applied the criterion of presumption of illegality to a merger by reference to the percentage market share held by the parties and to the concentration ratio of the enterprises in the market. In the same decision the Court held that the unfavourable anti-competitive effects of a merger could not be offset by any favourable economic consequences they might have. In subsequent decisions, these principles have become essential factors in determining whether a merger is likely to lessen competition substantially. There is only one exception to these principles - the failing company defence. The Merger Guidelines of the Department of Justice repeat the criteria laid down by the Supreme Court. They constitute merely a statement of the Department's current policy and are subject to revision in the light of changes in the enforcement of the anti-trust laws. The Guidelines indicate that the Department of Justice will ordinarily challenge horizontal mergers when the market shares of the acquiring and acquired firms are at a certain level (3). The market shares laid down are relatively low as can be seen, for example, from the fact that the Department indicates that it will challenge a merger if the acquiring firm pos-

---

1) United States v. Brown Shoe Company. Decree of 25th June, 1962 (370 U.S. 294).

2) United States v. Philadelphia National Bank. Decree of 1963 (374 U.S. 321).

3) Market shares are not the only relevant factor; account is also taken of factors such as the industry's tendency towards concentration, the degree of concentration, previous acquisitions of the firms wishing to merge and barriers to entry to the particular industry concerned.

sesses 4 per cent of the market and the acquired firm 4 per cent or more of the same market (1).

63.   Concerning vertical mergers (2), the Supreme Court has not laid down standards in terms of market shares and concentration ratios as it has done for horizontal mergers. In the cases United States v. E.I. Dupont de Nemours & Co. (3) and United States v. Brown Shoe (4), the Court held that the foreclosure of competing suppliers of the acquiring firm from the retail outlets offered by the acquired firm was the relevant anti-competitive effect. In the Guidelines, the Department of Justice defined its policy on vertical mergers, primarily in terms of the market shares held by the merging firms and conditions of entry to the market prior to the merger. Thus, the Department states that it will ordinarily challenge a merger or a series of mergers between a supplying firm, accounting for approximately 10 per cent or more of the sales, in its market, and one or more purchasing firms, accounting in toto for approximately 6 per cent or more of total purchases in that market, unless it clearly appears that there are no significant barriers to entry into the same business as the purchasing firm or firms.

64.   In addition, when a product supplied by one of the merging firms is a significant feature or ingredient of the end product manufactured by the purchasing firm and its competitors, the Department of Justice will ordinarily challenge a merger or series of mergers between a supplying firm accounting for approximately 20 per cent or more of the sales in its market and a purchasing firm or firms accounting in toto for approximately 10 per cent or more of the sales in the market in which it sells the product whose manufacture requires the supplying firm's product.

65.   Moreover, apart from the market share tests, the Department will challenge acquisitions of suppliers or customers by major firms in an industry in which :

i) there has been or is developing a significant trend towards vertical integration by merger such that the trend, if unchallenged, would probably raise barriers to entry or impose a competitive disadvantage on unintegrated or partly integrated firms; and

ii) it does not clearly appear that the particular acquisition will result in significant economies of production or distribution unrelated to advertising or other promotional economies.

1) The market shares causing intervention by the Department of Justice are given in detail in "Market Power and the Law", OECD, 1970, paragraphs 138-144.

2) See "Market Power and the Law", paragraphs 144-151 for further details.

3) 353 U.S. 586 (1957).

4) 370 U.S. 294 (1962).

66.   A recent decision of the Supreme Court in the case of "Ford Motor Co. v. United States" (1) lays down very clearly how the antitrust regulations are to be applied to vertical mergers. In 1961 Ford had purchased the Electric Autolite Company which controlled 15 per cent of the market for sparking plugs. The Court found the merger unlawful because a vertical merger of customer and supplier deprived rivals of the opportunity to compete in supplying Ford. In its opinion the Court stated that a merger was not saved from illegality because "on some ultimate reckoning of social or economic debits and credits, it may be deemed beneficial. A value choice of such magnitude is beyond the ordinary limits of judicial competence and in any event has been made for us already, by Congress when it enacted the amended paragraph 7. Congress determined to preserve our traditionally competitive economy. It therefore proscribed anti-competitive mergers, the benign and the malignant alike, fully aware, we must assume, that some price might have to be paid".

67.   With regard to <u>conglomerate mergers</u>, the three most significant potential anti-competitive effects discussed in the cases are (i) creation of a market structure conducive to reciprocal dealing; (ii) elimination of significant potential competition; (iii) entrenchment of the market position of the dominant or leading firm in a concentrated industry. The first aspect was dealt with by the Supreme Court in F.T.C. v. Consolidated Food Corporation (2). The Supreme Court held that the creation of reciprocity power with the possibility of substantial lessening of competition would be sufficient to render a merger illegal. Under its Merger Guidelines the Department of Justice will ordinarily challenge any merger which creates "a significant danger of reciprocal buying" (3). Such a danger is normally considered to be present "whenever approximately 15 per cent or more of the total purchase in a market in which one of the merging firms' ('the selling firm') sales are accounted for by firms which also make substantial sales in markets where the other merging firm ('the buying firm') is both a substantial buyer and a more substantial buyer than all or most of the competitors of the selling firm". In addition, the Department will ordinarily challenge "(i) any merger undertaken for the purpose of facilitating the creation of reciprocal buying arrangements, and (ii) any merger creating the possibility of any substantial reciprocal buying where one (or both) of the merging firms has within the recent past, or the merged firm has after consummation of the merger, actually engaged in reciprocal buying in the product markets in which the possibility of reciprocal buying has been created" (4).

1) Ford Motor Co. v. United States, 405 U.S. 562 (1972).
2) 380 U.S. 592, 1965 Trade Cases, paragraph 71.432.
3) Guidelines, No. 19.
4) Idem.

68.  In a number of recent cases (1) the Supreme Court has enunciated the principle that a conglomerate merger is illegal when it is likely to eliminate significant inter-product or inter-market potential competition between the firms. In other words, the decisions established that a merger may be considered to lessen competition substantially if one of the merging parties is a potential competitor of the other, situated at the edge of the relevant market and likely to enter that market at some time. In its Merger Guidelines, the Department of Justice has taken account of this case law and has stated that it will challenge (2) any merger between one of the most likely entrants and :

    i) any firm with approximately 25 per cent or more of the market;

   ii) one of the two largest firms in a market in which the shares of the two largest firms amount to approximately 50 per cent or more;

  iii) one of the four largest firms in a market in which the shares of the eight largest firms amount to approximately 75 per cent or more, provided that the merging firms' share of the market amounts to approximately 10 per cent or more; or

  iv) one of the eight largest firms in the market in which the share of these firms amount to approximately 75 per cent or more, provided either (a) the merging firms' share of the market is not insubstantial and there are more than one or two likely entrants into the market or (b) the merging firm is a rapidly growing firm.

69.  In its Merger Guidelines the Department of Justice has indicated that it may bring suit against a conglomerate merger where an acquisition of a leading firm in a relatively concentrated or rapidly concentrating market may serve to entrench or increase the market power of that firm or raise barriers to entry in that market. Examples of this type of merger include : (i) a merger which produces a very large disparity in absolute size between the merged firm and the largest remaining firms in the relevant markets, (ii) a merger of firms producing related products which may induce purchasers, concerned about the merged firm's possible use of leverage, to buy products of the merged firm rather than those of competitors, and (iii) a merger which may enhance the ability of the merged firm to increase product differentiation in the relevant markets (3).

---

1) United States v. El Paso Natural Gas Company, 376 U.S. 651 (1964) F.T.C. v. Proctor & Gamble Co., 386 U.S. 568 (1967).

2) Merger Guidelines, No. 18.

3) The F.T.C. appears to follow approximately the same policies. See F.T.C. v. Proctor & Gamble Co., 386 U.S. 568 (1967); Reynolds Metals v. F.T.C., 309 F. 2d 223 (D.C. Cir. 1962).

70.   In Japan, mergers are controlled by the Act concerning prohibition of private monopoly and maintenance of fair trade. Mergers, transfers of business, inter-company stockholdings and interlocking directorates are prohibited when their effect may be to restrain competition substantially in any particular field of trade or where unfair business practices have been employed. A prior reporting system applies to mergers and transfers of business and, where the Fair Trade Commission intends to take action against any merger or transfer of business, it must do so within thirty days after the report has been filed (a sixty day extension may be available with the consent of the companies concerned). As regards inter-company stockholdings and interlocking directorates, a system of post-notification to the Fair Trade Commission is applied to companies whose assets exceed a certain level (in the case of stockholdings, 500 million yen for the stockholding  company's assets and in the case of interlocking directorates, 500 million yen for either company's assets). In addition, it is illegal for a financial company to hold stock in a Japanese company in excess of 10 per cent of its total stock and the establishment of a holding company whose principal business is to control the business activities of companies in Japan is prohibited.

71.   In Japan there are no guidelines for assessing mergers and a case-by-case investigation is undertaken for proposed mergers. There has been only one merger case, the merger between the Yawata Iron and Steel Co. Ltd. and the Fuji Iron and Steel Co., Ltd. against which legal proceedings have been taken under Section 15 of the Anti-Monopoly Act. The Fair Trade Commission issued a consent decision approving the merger on the condition that certain assets and know-how were sold to other steel producers. These measures were designed to eliminate the dominant position of the merged firm. In that decision, the Fair Trade Commission gave its interpretation as follows.

72.   Within the meaning of Section 15 of the Anti-Monopoly Act, a merger may have the effect of substantially restraining competition in a particular field of trade when the market structure as compared with that prevailing prior to the merger becomes non-competitive and where, as a result, a particular entrepreneur may attain a controlling position on the market. If an entrepreneur has come to monopolize a market or has come to acquire the power to exert such a degree of influence by this own will upon price, quality, quantity, and various other conditions of transactions that  his competitors become unable to carry on their business activities independently, the entrepreneur shall be regarded as one attaining a controlling position on the market.

73.   Whether or not a market controlling position is created with respect to a particular entrepreneur is determined  by taking  various

economic conditions into consideration, including the existing situation in the industry sector to which the companies involved in the proposed merger belong, the market shares in each field of trade, the respective circumstances of suppliers and users, the existence or non-existence of imports or substitutes and the difficulty of entry, etc.

74. In the <u>United Kingdom</u>, the Department of Prices and Consumer Protection has power to refer mergers or proposed mergers to the Monopolies and Mergers Commission for investigation and report :
   a) where the merger would lead to or strengthen a "monopoly", (i.e. a situation where one quarter or more of any trade was in the hands of one person or group); or
   b) where the gross value of the assets taken over or to be taken over exceeds £ 5 million.

The Commission are required to report whether the merger operates or may be expected to operate against the public interest. The Department have power to prohibit mergers and (with the consent of Parliament) to dissolve mergers which the Commission have found to operate against the public interest. There is special provision for the control of newspaper mergers.

75. In practice, while a large number of mergers were considered by the Board of Trade (now the Department of Prices and Consumer Protection) (1), only a few of these were referred to the Monopolies Commission. It should be mentioned, however, that in a number of important cases the Board of Trade decided not to refer the merger to the Monopolies Commission after receiving assurances from the firms involved as to their future behaviour. The Monopolies Commission found that a few mergers (one third of the cases submitted to it) would operate against the public interest. However, in only one of these did the Board of Trade need to make an order prohibiting the merger (2). In the other cases the parties gave undertakings not to proceed with their merger proposals following an unfavourable opinion by the Commission.

76. On the occasion of its reports on the proposed mergers concerning Rank Organisation/De La Rue and Unilever/Allied Breweries, the Monopolies Commission stated its position in a short report entitled "General Observations on Mergers". The report noted that while the actual number of take-overs in the United Kingdom had tended to decline since 1965, these operations now involved much larger enterprises than before. The Commission felt, however, that the take-over movement had not led to the growth of firms whose size in absolute terms raised serious problems as regards the public interest.

---

1) See "Mergers - A Guide to Board of Trade Practice", London, 1969.
2) This was in the Rank Organisation/De La Rue case.

77.     Concerning the effects of the different forms of merger on competition, the Commission observed that conglomerate mergers were less
likely to have anti-competitive effects than horizontal or vertical
mergers and that it was, therefore, just as important to assess their
effects on efficiency as on competition. The Commission recommended
that more complete financial information should be provided by firms
undertaking mergers and that the Board of Trade should collect and
publish more statistical and general information, particularly about
the extent and form of any diversification involved.

78.     Within the European Communities, prior control of concentrations
was confined, until very recently, to the coal and steel sectors. This
control was exercised under Article 66 of the Treaty establishing the
European Coal and Steel Community (ECSC), which provides that concentrations require prior authorisation by the Commission of the European
Communities (High Authority).

79.     A concentration exists, within the meaning of Article 66 (1),
when a person or an enterprise or a group of persons or enterprises
acquires the power to control another enterprise. The factors determining control have been defined in Decision No. 24/54 of 6th May, 1954(1).

80.     Pursuant to Article 66 (2) authorisation must be granted if the
enterprises involved do not acquire the power to determine prices, to
control or restrict production or distribution or to prevent the maintenance of effective competition in a substantial part of the market
for the products concerned (2).

81.     Thus, when examining such an operation the Commission, contrary
to the provisions of Article 65 of the ECSC Treaty which governs agree-
ments, concerted practices etc., must not take into account only the
position held by the parties concerned on the market in question.
Consequently, it is not empowered to decide whether a particular concentration would or would not promote rationalisation of production,
sales or purchases.

82.     So as to ensure a sufficient degree of competition, the Commission may make its authorisation subject to certain conditions which
must be observed by the parties concerned. In this way, the Commission
frequently has recourse to the possibility, in order to keep the large
groups separate, of prohibiting personal relationships between them.
It may be estimated that more than 200 decisions have been taken under
Article 66.

---

1) Official Journal of the ECSC of 11th May, 1954.

2) See the communication of the Commission dealing with the structure
   of the steel industry in the European Communities. Official Journal
   of the European Communities, 30th January, 1970.

83.    Furthermore, the Commission of the European Communities has for
the first time given a decision under Article 86 of the Treaty of Rome
on a concentration in the light metal containers sector (the Continental Can Case) (1), which was deemed to be against the law because it
deprived users in a substantial part of the Common Market of their freedom of choice. This decision confirms the interpretation of Article 86
which the Commission has given previously, namely that the acquisition
by a market-dominating enterprise of another enterprise, involving the
virtual elimination of competition in certain products over a substantial part of the Common Market, is an abuse of its market-dominating position. The parties to the merger took the case to the European
Court of Justice.

84.    In its judgment of 21st February, 1973, the Court confirmed the
Commission's interpretation of Article 86 as to the applicability of
this Article to certain concentrations.

85.    Taking into account the spirit, disposition and terms of Article
86 in the system and objectives of the Treaty, the Court noted that
the latter is based on regulations ensuring that competition is not
distorted or eliminated in the Common Market. It observed that the
prohibition of cartels laid down in Article 85 would be meaningless
if Article 86 allowed these practices to become lawful when they took
place within a concentration of enterprises. Such a contradiction would
undermine the rules of competition in such a way as to compromise the
effective working of the Common Market. The Court accordingly decided
that there was abuse when "an enterprise in a dominant position strengthened this position to the point where the degree of domination thus
achieved hampered competition to an appreciable extent, i.e. would
leave only enterprises depending, in their action, on the dominant
enterprise".

86.    The Court quashed the decision of the Commission, however, on the
grounds that the latter had not sufficiently defined the market in
question. The Court indicated in this respect that "in order to be
regarded as constituting a separate market, the products in question
must be distinguished not only by the mere fact that they are used for
the packaging of certain products, but also by the special characteristics  of production making them suitable specifically for this purpose".

87.    The trend towards mergers would, if it were to continue unchecked,
constitute a threat to the maintenance of undistorted competition within the Common Market. It is recalled that the Final Declaration of the
Paris Summit Conference acknowledged that the Community should work out
appropriate rules to ensure that merger operations involving enterprises established in the Community are in harmony with the Community's
economic and social objectives.

1) Official Journal No. L7/72 of 8th January, 1972.

88.    Accordingly the Commission submitted a proposal to the Council
for a regulation for the surveillance of concentration operations,
based on Articles 87 and 235 of the EEC Treaty, including the following provisions :
   a) mergers between enterprises are incompatible with the Common
      Market if such mergers are liable to affect trade between
      Member States and if thereby the merging enterprises acquire
      or enhance their capability to hinder effective competition;
   b) the foregoing should not apply to concentrations which do not
      exceed specified minimum quantitative criteria;
   c) the regulation should provide for exemption from a ruling of
      incompatibility in the case of merger operations which are
      necessary for the attaining of a priority Community objective;
   d) major merger operations involving enterprises which together
      have a total turnover of 1,000 million units of account or more
      should be notified in advance and there should be a three-month
      suspension period during which the Commission may start pro-
      ceedings. If the Commission does not start proceedings in res-
      pect of a proposed merger within such three months, the merger
      operation should be taken to be unobjectionable. If proceedings
      are started, a Commission decision should be given within nine
      months;
   e) any legal steps taken in connection with the merger operation
      in question should not be regarded as void, even if the merger
      is ruled to be incompatible with the Common Market.

89.    The proposed regulation is based on the principle of individual
case-by-case assessment of proposed mergers to ascertain their compatibility with Community objectives. The exemption provisions make it
possible to allow for appropriate requirements of industrial, technological, social or regional policies to be implemented at Community
level.


## III. CRITERIA USED IN TAKING ACTION AGAINST MERGER OPERATIONS

90.    The brief description given above of the action against merger
operations taken by some Member countries shows that the criteria used
to judge the legality of a merger vary from one Member country to another.

91.    In Canada, mergers whereby competition is or is likely to be
lessened to the detriment or against the interest of the public are
prohibited by criminal law. The courts have interpreted the law as
requiring the creation of a virtual monopoly. However, jurisprudence
on other provisions of the Combines Investigation Act has indicated

some difference of opinion with respect to the virtual monopoly test. In his administration of the Act, the Director of Investigation and Research is prepared to explore merger situations which, on the best judgement he can form from the language of the Statute, raise proper issues for the appellate courts to determine.

92.    In the United States, the decisive criterion is the probability of substantial lessening of competition, because it is considered that the maintenance of vigorous competition is in the long run beneficial to consumers and to industry itself and that it is the surest protection of the public interest. In sectors regulated by special laws (transport, banks, etc.) the Supreme Court has interpreted Congress' intent to be that expert administrative tribunals, having considered the competitive objections to a merger submitted beforehand for approval, may nevertheless conclude that the transaction's benefits in achieving the special goals of the Regulatory Act should outweigh the adverse effect on competition it may have. The efficiency concept is not recognised as a justification by the antitrust laws and by the courts for major horizontal or vertical mergers, since it is assumed that appropriate size and efficiency can be achieved by internal growth, by mergers with smaller firms, or joint arrangements short of merger, such as computer timesharing. Efficiency may be evaluated from several different standpoints and may refer to different stages of production or distribution, depending on whether size or productive units, research expenditure or marketing is envisaged. As regards technology, efficiency is considered most likely to be achieved when keen competition exists and when research is undertaken by a substantial number of independent research units (which is why the joint agreement among automobile manufacturers controlling commercial exploitation of anti-pollution devices was condemned). However,  there is no general ban in American antitrust law on joint research.

93.    In Japan, the criterion employed is that of substantial restraint of competition. In the Anti-Monopoly Act, it is considered that promoting free and fair competition has the effect of stimulating the initiative of enterpreneurs, encouraging business activities of enterprises, heightening the level of employment and people's real income, and thereby promoting the democratic and wholesome development of the national economy as well as assuring the interests of consumers in general. In practice, greater efficiency is advocated by the merging parties whereas the antitrust authorities, for their part, concentrate upon the restraint of competition resulting from the merger.

94.    In Germany, the decisive criterion is the creation or strengthening of a market dominating position which comes close to the criterion of lessening of competition. The Cartel Authority has to trade off the disadvantages of market dominance against any improvements

in competitive conditions brought about by the merger. As the merging parties must prove that the merger will have beneficial effects the onus is not upon the Cartel Authority to make a trade-off analysis in each case.

95.    In the <u>United Kingdom</u>, attention is first given to the public interest and competition is considered as one important aspect of this. But efficiency is also taken into account when deciding whether the merger is compatible with the public interest. Since greater efficiency may be one of the objectives sought by the parties to the merger, the authorities consider that they have as much interest in the merger  as the firms themselves. Thus a study of the efficiency of the merger falls within the wide framework of the public interest criterion which has been adopted in the United Kingdom. In addition, the efficiency of a merger is assessed by reference to a market, which might in some cases be the whole world, and by reference to the competitiveness of the parties to the merger on this market. As a result improved international competitiveness is often a determining factor in approving a merger.

96.    In conclusion, lessening of competition and efficiency are the two main criteria used in Member countries for judging the economic effects of mergers, although the emphasis given to each varies from one Member country to another. Moreover, some Member countries take into account, to varying extents, other economic considerations such as the effects of the merger on employment or on the balance of payments. The differences of emphasis noted are not only the result of different economic structures and market sizes in Member countries but also of the adoption of different economic philosophies.

97.    In practice, the problem of the size of enterprises is closely related to that of the criteria to apply in considering mergers. Despite differences between Member countries (e.g. some countries consider the market shares held by the merging enterprises rather than their sizes), large size by itself cannot serve as a yardstick to prove that a particular merger is against the general interest. However, below limits which may vary from one country to another, the size of the firms involved in a merger serves to show that the general interest would not be prejudiced if a merger takes place between enterprises which do not have sufficient size to affect competition.


IV. WORKING PRINCIPLES OF SYSTEMS OF MERGER CONTROL


98.    The way in which a system of merger control operates depends mainly on the criterion used in judging whether mergers are legally acceptable, the choice of criterion depending in turn on the reasons for establishing the system. Although these reasons have been explained

in detail in Chapter I of this study devoted to the economic aspects, it may be useful to stress that most mergers between relatively un-important enterprises have no harmful effect on the general interest, because their effects on competition are extremely slight, so that it is unnecessary to take action against them under restrictive business practices legislation. On the other hand, there are a few mergers which, while they may lead to economies of scale and to a better uti-lisation of resources, may give rise to objections from the point of view of competition or the public interest, because they increase concentration and the economic power of the enterprises concerned. It is only mergers of this kind against which action is taken under res-trictive business practices legislation.

99.     Accordingly, merger control can be linked either to the size of enterprises or to the extent to which they dominate a market or to a lessening of competition. A merger is only subject to controls if the combined assets or turnover involved, the economic structure or the conditions of the market, or the state of competition show that it might appreciably limit competition or be against the public interest (1). The above factors determine, as it were, the general conditions governing the enforcement of a system of merger control and these con-ditions vary widely from one Member country to another, as described in the section dealing with the legal status of mergers in Member countries (paragraphs 54 to 89 above).

100.    The specific reasons given in a particular country for control-ling mergers, and the country's general policy on competition, influ-ence the choice of the criteria used in judging mergers. Either the substantial lessening of competition which may result from a merger is considered in itself to be a sufficient criterion or other criteria such as the effects on the balance of payments, employment, prices, economies of scale etc. are regarded as equally important.

101.    In the latter case it will be necessary to draw up a regular balance sheet for the merger by assessing the favourable or unfavour-able effects which it may have in the short or longer term. In prac-tice, that concept seems to favour a system of control either by admin-istrative authorities or by special courts because it entails many elements requiring particular economic expertise such as the setting of economic priorities which would be demanding too much from the regular courts. The "lessening of competition approach", on the other hand, may be applied by the regular courts as well as by the admin-istrative authorities or special courts.

---

1) Under United States' law and as expressed in the Department of Justice's Guidelines a merger may be challenged because it elimi-nates a single small firm of unique importance or independence.

102.    The respective merits of judicial versus administrative control
of mergers are frequently the subject of controversy. The Committee
did not consider it useful or necessary to enter into this controver-
sial area, the solution to which depends on a host of historical, political and legal circumstances, but rather stressed the desirable features which any system whether judicial, administrative or mixed should
incorporate in order to work effectively.

103.    In the first place there is the essential requirement that any
decision on a proposed or consummated merger should be reached quickly
for the sake of the enterprises involved. This is because on the one
hand undue delay might result in an economically justifiable merger
being called off or may hold up the integration of an already completed
merger which is going to be allowed in any event. On the other hand,
if it is true that when a proposed merger is prohibited no serious un-
winding operations are necessary, this is not the case for already
completed mergers. This dilemma has often led the authorities in essentially judicial systems where the problem arises most acutely (although
it is also present in administrative systems) to institute pre-merger
notification procedures or consultations or to issue guidelines for
applying the legislation. Moreover in the United States a preliminary
injunction may be issued by the courts to prevent a proposed merger
going ahead until a final judgement is rendered by the courts if the
latter conclude that there is a reasonable probability that the merger
is illegal.

104.    Secondly, it follows from this that the laying down of reasonable time limits for considering mergers and the appropriate timing
of actions against mergers are also essential for an efficient merger
control system. This is relevant both in a system of advance clearance
(Japan, ECSC, the United Kingdom for newspaper mergers, and Germany
for large mergers) and in a system of post intervention as applied in
Canada, in the United Kingdom and in the United States and, to the
extent that pre-merger clearance is not applicable, in Japan and in
Germany. The absence of a reasonable time limit for bringing an action
against a merger must create in most cases not only insecurity for the
enterprises involved but also serious practical difficulties in imple-
menting a subsequent dissolution. In this connection the advance clearance of a proposed merger, whether of a compulsory or of a more informal
character has many advantages, notably by giving an assurance to the
firms involved that if a merger is not contested within the prescribed
time limit, it will be allowed to proceed and will not subsequently
be challenged. Although informal clearance given in such cases is neither binding on the administration nor on the courts, it seems that in
practice in only very rare cases is action taken by the administration
contrary to its prior opinion given to the parties. With regard to the

time period for making a preliminary administrative investigation, it varies within the various Member countries from 30 days to a few months. In Japan this period is normally 30 days, although a further 60-day extension is allowed with the consent of the merging parties. In the United Kingdom, for all except newspaper mergers, the Department of Prices and Consumer Protection decides within three weeks of the merger announcement whether to refer the matter to the Monopolies and Mergers Commission, which normally takes three months to make its report (a maximum of six months is provided in the legislation). In the United States the companies may be asked to postpone a merger while the Antitrust Division or FTC considers whether action should be taken. In Germany, on the other hand, the Federal Cartel Office has four months after notification of proposed mergers to decide whether to take action to prevent the merger and the Minister of Economic Affairs a further four months to consider whether to grant a special exemption. In the case of post-merger control, the Federal Cartel Office has to decide within a one-year time limit.

105. The third requirement of an effective merger control system is that some pre-merger informal or formal notification or consultation procedure should be available for the parties to permit both them and the authorities to assess the acceptability of a merger before it is completed.

106. The most extensive notification scheme is found in Japan, where all mergers, regardless of size (including service industry mergers) and transfers of business have to be notified to the Fair Trade Commission. In Germany, advance notification is required when sales proceeds of D.M. 1 billion or more are reached by at least two enterprises involved in the merger during the year preceding it. In the United States, a reporting requirement exists for very large mergers under the Federal Trade Commission Regulations. This, however, applies only to mergers and acquisitions where the assets of the acquiring company exceed $250 million and those of the acquired company exceed $10 million or where a new company is formed whose assets exceed $250 million. Meanwhile, it should be stressed that Germany, Canada, Spain and Sweden keep mergers registers or a list of mergers notified.

107. A system of compulsory notification is helpful for a system demanding advance clearance of proposed mergers (see paragraph 54 above); moreover it is useful for general inquiries into the trend of concentration. However, for systems involving control after merger, prior notification is less important.

108. Fourthly, in order to separate substantial from unimportant mergers, it seems that quantifiable criteria may be desirable whether they are laid down in regulations under the relevant legislation or sanctioned by administrative practice. Such criteria may take the form

of legally prescribed market shares, sales, size of assets or number of employees of the merging firms which must be fulfilled before the merger falls to be examined or they may take the form of guidelines or rules based on case law which lay down the conditions under which mergers may be illegal. Formal requirements of this kind are not the complete answer to the prevention of undesirable mergers in that they do not provide a definition of the relevant market nor do they permit action against all potentially undesirable mergers - for example, those below the prescribed limits or those involving companies with unique features. However, for practical purposes quantifiable criteria would seem desirable to avoid the heavy administrative costs involved in scrutinising every merger regardless of its size.

109.    All this leads to the final and most difficult element of an ideal merger control system - the choice of criteria for determining whether or on what terms a particular merger should be allowed . Essentially this choice is influenced by the basic attitudes of Member countries towards competition which in turn may be influenced by the country's size, industrial structure, state of economic development and position in relation to foreign trade. Where vigorous competition is considered to be the primary goal of economic policy, any action tending to concentrate the competitive structure of a particular industry may be held to be harmful in itself, while, if it is not, a system of merger control based on the avoidance of monopoly and prevention of abuse of oligopoly power may be sufficient. In practice however, as this chapter has indicated, the merger control systems in operation in Member countries are not as different as this brief description of alternative criteria would seem to indicate. Whatever criteria are used for judging mergers, the antitrust authorities, once they have the power by administrative or judicial means to prevent a merger in certain circumstances, may also authorise it on condition that the parties agree to provide guarantees or take precautions to safeguard the public interest and ensure adequate competition. This is done in the United States by means of consent decrees and in regulated industries, and in the European Communities and Japan in the decisions issued by the competent administrative body. Moreover, it should be noted that some merger control policies lead not so much to banning mergers as to authorising them on certain conditions designed to guarantee that the economic power resulting from the merger will be exercised in a way conducive to the public interest. From this point of view, controls on the formation of mergers are on a par with measures to prevent abuses by market-dominating enterprises and monopolies. These two forms of control are mutually complementary and help to prevent exploitation of consumers or abuse of competitors.

Chapter III

INTERNATIONAL MERGERS

## Introduction

110.    The characteristic which distinguishes the international merger from the domestic merger discussed in Chapter I is that they are
one of the means by which foreign direct investment may be implemented,
and it is this which makes them of special concern. Therefore, before
considering the reasons for, and the effects of, international mergers
it would be valuable to examine some of the main issues which arise
out of foreign investment. There are 3 principal areas of concern :
  a) The possibility that the foreign firm involves the host Govern-
       ment in a loss of control or sovereignty.
  b) The possibility that the transaction would create capital or
     · revenue effects considered undesirable.
  c) The competitive effects.
The  first  2 issues are  not directly related to competition policy, and while they may be the most important in some countries because
of the very high degree of foreign ownership, attention in this chapter
will be confined to the competitive effects. This is not to suggest
that the political effects are of no concern to policies about competition, they may well be of the first order of importance, but the
concern in this chapter is to identify the economic effects insofar
as these may be relevant to a policy about mergers.

111.    A recent analysis, put in terms of relevance for competition
policies, is that of Caves (1) who emphasizes the 2 important aspects
of the phenomenon : that it normally results in the net transfer of
the real capital from one country to another; and that it represents
entry into a national industry by a firm established in the foreign
market. It follows directly from these that such investment will have
efficiency and market power consequences and hence the analysis developed in Chapter I is of use for assessing the consequences.

112.    The size of a foreign firm seeking to acquire a firm in another
country, as well as the size of the acquired firm, will likely have
relevance to analysis of the consequences of the transaction. This is

---

1) "International Corporations - The Industrial Economies of Foreign
   Investment" article published in Economica, Volume 38, 1971.

especially so if the acquisition is in the nature of a product or market extension merger. Then, it will generally be true that the larger the foreign firm, the more likely it is to be a significant potential entrant by way of de novo entry or foothold acquisition into the national economy of the acquired firm. Also, the larger the domestic firm, the more likely that it might be a potential entrant into the foreign market, and the more likely that there are smaller firms which the foreign firm could use for a foothold merger. Lastly, the size of the acquiring and acquired firm may be relevant in predicting whether the merged company would be likely to achieve an undesirable competitive dominance in any market. This is not to say that the competitive effect of the acquisition should be measured solely or even primarily according to the size of the firms. It is simply an observation that as the size of the acquiring and the acquired firms becomes larger, it is more likely that anti-competitive consequences will result from the proposed transaction.

113. In terms of competition policy, the consequences of any such transaction must be measured by its effect upon competition and not by extraneous considerations such as whether foreign direct investment is thought desirable or undesirable in terms of other policies of the Member countries. Ideally, policies to limit or encourage foreign direct investment should be clearly distinguished from policies concerning the possible anti-competitive effects of mergers or acquisitions.

## Motives for International Mergers

114. Foreign direct investment, although it may take a variety of organisational forms, represents for the outward investing firm either a horizontal, a vertical or a diversified extension of its existing activities. While there are many factors which stimulate international merger activity and other forms of foreign direct investment it may be stated, for example, that horizontal mergers may be encouraged by a desire to enter protected markets, vertical mergers may be fostered by lower costs of production and both types of merger may be encouraged by Government financial incentives. Available evidence suggests that the predominant extensions will be horizontal and vertical, and that the diversified will be comparatively rare (1). Horizontal extensions are explained in terms of the possession by the firm of some special asset such as, amongst other things, a patented invention or a differentiated product. For such extensions to be successful 2 conditions must be satisfied : that the special asset has the character of "a public good" within the firm, that is to say that it may be successfully transferred between markets at little or no cost to the firm; and secondly, the potential return in the foreign market must depend

---

1) See, for example, Caves, op. cit.

46

in part, at least, upon local production. The foreign investor is, of course, at a disadvantage compared with national firms because they have a stock of knowledge and experience of economic, social, legal and cultural conditions which he does not have. However, he will expect that the possession of his special asset will more than offset this disadvantage, and that local production would yield a higher return than the alternatives of licensing or exporting. This leads to the conclusion that the special asset creates some form of product differentiation which may in the right circumstances, enable the firm to earn higher than normal profits. It therefore suggests that horizontal direct investment will both arise from and flow into those industries where product differentiation advantages are important and where there are also substantial entry barriers.

115.    There is some evidence which would support the suggestion made above. For example Steuer in "The Impact of Foreign Direct Investment on the United Kingdom", HMSO, 1973, has found that highly concentrated industries also have a high degree of concentration of foreign ownership and that in terms of absolute size, enterprises which engage in international mergers are large. Also, in the United States, Caves has found a high rank correlation between the extent of product differentiation and the proportion for firms in an industry having foreign subsidiaries. Product differentiation is not, of course, the only factor explaining horizontal direct foreign investment; other factors can also be important, such as the influence of tariff and non-tariff barriers, but there is no doubt that it is a major factor accounting for such flows.

116.    The explanation offered by Caves for vertical direct foreign investment stresses the motives of securing supplies of raw materials by backward integration, and the avoidance of oligopolistic risk and the erection of entry barriers where vertical integration occurs amongst the more industrialised countries. These lead to the conclusion that high concentration is also likely to be a feature of the market of the firms making such investments, and that such firms are also likely to be large in size.

Extent of International Mergers

117.    Statistics on the number and size of international mergers are available in some Member countries although they are essentially fragmentary, being based mainly on often imperfect press information. Any firm quantification of the extent of international mergers is difficult mainly due to the absence of merger control provisions or reporting procedures which enable official statistics to be compiled.

118.    Figures are available in Canada, Germany, Sweden, the Netherlands, the United Kingdom and the European Communities. In Canada the

Director of Investigation and Research has maintained since 196,
register in which an attempt is made to record all mergers that have
taken place in those sectors of Canadian industry subject to the Combines Investigation Act and which have been reported in the press.
Table 1 sets out the total number of acquisitions during the period
1960-1973 and a breakdown of these acquisitions to indicate those involving a known foreign owned or controlled acquiring company and those
involving a company not known to be foreign owned or controlled (1).

Table 1

NO. OF MERGERS RECORDED IN CANADA, BY YEAR

| Year | (a) Foreign(2) | (b) Domestic(3) | (c) Total | (a) as % of (c) |
|------|------|------|------|------|
| 1960 | 93 | 110 | 203 | 46% |
| 1961 | 86 | 152 | 238 | 36% |
| 1962 | 79 | 106 | 185 | 43% |
| 1963 | 41 | 88 | 129 | 32% |
| 1964 | 80 | 124 | 204 | 39% |
| 1965 | 78 | 157 | 235 | 33% |
| 1966 | 80 | 123 | 203 | 39% |
| 1967 | 85 | 143 | 228 | 37% |
| 1968 | 163 | 239 | 402 | 41% |
| 1969 | 168 | 336 | 504 | 36% |
| 1970 | 162 | 265 | 427 | 39% |
| 1971 | 143 | 245 | 388 | 37% |
| 1972 | 127 | 302 | 429 | 30% |
| 1973 | 100(4) | 252(4) | 352(4) | 28% |

119.    It is difficult to draw any firm conclusions on the trend of
international mergers (as defined in the Canadian statistics) from
the figures on number of acquisitions. The figures do show however that
international mergers account for a far higher proportion of total mergers in Canada than in other countries for which data are available.
Over this 14 year period international mergers averaged 36 per cent of
all recorded mergers in Canada. These figures do not, however, indicate

1) Source : Report of the Director of Investigation and Research,
   Combines Investigation Act, for the year ended 31st March, 1973,
   p.  51 and subsequently revised by the Canadian Delegation to OECD.

2) Acquisitions involving a known foreign owned or controlled acquiring company (the nationality of the controlling interest in the
   acquired company prior to the merger could have been foreign or
   Canadian).

3) Acquisitions involving an acquired company not known to be foreign
   owned or controlled (the nationality of the controlling interest
   in the acquired company prior to the merger could have been foreign
   or Canadian).

4) Preliminary.

the relative importance of foreign mergers either in terms of the
assets acquired by foreign acquiring firms in relation to domestic
acquiring firms or in relation to specific sectors. Rosenbluth (1)
attempted to investigate these relationships for the years 1945-1961
from data provided by the Director of Investigation and Research.
The results of his investigation suggested that foreign firms as a
whole were responsible for a disproportionately high amount of merger
activity in selected industries (2) compared with domestic firms. He
also detected a significant trend in these industries in that the
percentage of Canadian control declined while the percentage of United
States control  increased somewhat and the percentage of capital controlled by other foreign interests increased more spectacularly.

120.    In _Sweden_, international mergers accounted for 8 per cent of
Swedish mergers in 1972. They accounted for 15 per cent in 1971, the
same as in 1969, but almost twice the share of mergers in 1970. In
1972 the foreign owned companies accounted for about 7 per cent of
total manufacturing output in Sweden (1967 : 5 per cent).

121. The chemical industry is the most foreign-dominated part of industry, 37 per cent (1970). In the electronic industry the corresponding share was 15 per cent, food industry 5 per cent, graphic industry
5 per cent, pulp and paper industry 2 per cent.

122.    The number of foreign purchases of Swedish enterprises or parts
of enterprises decreased somewhat during the year 1972 in comparison
with 1971. In all, 29 purchases have been noted for 1972 where the
buying enterprises were foreign-owned. In 1971 the corresponding number
was 37. Of the 29 enterprises acquired in 1972 :

        1 had more than 2,000 employees,
        1  "     300-399          "    ,
        1  "     200-299          "    ,
        3  "     100-199          "    ,
        23 "       0-99           "    .

123.    The most important foreign purchase that took place in 1972 was
the British company Cavenham Ltd's acquisition of the Swedish food
enterprise AB Felix. Second was Peugeot SA's acquisition of its Swedish
general representative, AB Gjestvang & Co.

124.    Among companies acquired were primary manufacturing companies
especially in the field of chemicals and mechanical engineering (9 and
6). After that followed electronics manufacturers (4) and food industries (3).

---

1) G. Rosenbluth, The Relation between Foreign Control and Concentration in Canadian Industry, Canadian Journal of Economies, February
   1970.

2) Manufacturing, petroleum and natural gas, mining and smelting, rail-
   ways, utilities, merchandising.

125.    In the Netherlands, the explanatory memorandum to the 1973 Bud-
get indicated the trend in the number of national and international
mergers in the Netherlands during the period 1966-1971. The figures show
an increase in the proportion of international mergers. Mergers with
foreign enterprises accounted for 17 per cent of the total in 1966, 19
per cent in 1967, 22 per cent in 1968, 29 per cent in 1969, 22 per cent
in 1970, 25 per cent in 1971 and 40 per cent in 1972 (1).

126.    In Germany, there were 16 "substantial" international mergers
in 1970 (foreign firms acquiring German firms) compared with 83 (excluding bank and insurance mergers) large purely domestic mergers, involving mergers where the acquired firm's assets amounted to at least DM
25 million (2). In 1971 17 "substantial" international mergers took
place compared with 49 large domestic mergers (3). In 1972, 11 mergers
out of 75 substantial mergers were international. A study covering all
mergers notified to the Federal Cartel Office from 1966 to the end of
1972 shows that most mergers were of a purely national character. Of
1,135 mergers 221 were international, i.e. approximately one-fifth.
The share of international mergers varied annually between 12 and 23
per cent. In 1973, 242 mergers were notified to the Federal Cartel
Office of which 75 involved foreign enterprises directly or indirectly.

127.    In the United Kingdom, the Mergers Panel, an inter-departmental
group which advises the Secretary of State on mergers, have considered
a number of proposed mergers which fall within the scope of the 1965
Act, 11 per cent of which involved acquisitions of United Kingdom companies by foreign enterprises. These are reported in Tables 2 and 3
below.

Table 2

ANALYSIS OF MERGERS CONSIDERED BY UNITED KINGDOM MERGERS PANEL

| Year | 1965 | 1966 | 1967 | 1968 | 1969 | 1970 | 1971 | 1972 | Cumulative Total |
|---|---|---|---|---|---|---|---|---|---|
| Total | 41 | 58 | 91 | 128 | 120 | 79 | 107 | 112 | 736 |
| Of which : acquired by a foreign company | 3 | 6 | 9 | 11 | 15 | 10 | 17 | 9 | 80 |
| % of Total | 7 | 10 | 10 | 9 | 12 | 13 | 16 | 8 | 11 |

1) The 1972 figures also include service industry mergers which were
   not included in the figures from 1966 to 1971.
2) Federal Cartel Office Annual Activity Report for 1970, Deutscher
   Bundestag, Drucksache VI/2380.
3) Federal Cartel Office Annuel Activity Report for 1972, Deutscher
   Bundestag, Drucksache 7/986.

Table 3

FOREIGN DIRECT INVESTMENT MERGERS ANALYSED
BY TYPE OF INTEGRATION 1965-1972

| Type | Number | Per cent |
|------|--------|----------|
| Horizontal | 67 | 84 |
| Vertical | 3 | 4 |
| Diversified | 10 | 12 |
| Total | 80 | 100 |

128.    Finally, in the <u>European Communities</u>, the Commission's second
report on competition policy contained statistics on international
operations within the Communities from 1966 to 1971 (1). These operations were broken down into 3 categories - acquisitions of minority
or majority shares in the capital of an enterprise by at least one
enterprise situated in another Member country; creation of joint subsidiaries in an E.E.C. Member country by at least 2 enterprises, one
of which is of a different nationality; and finally creation of individual subsidiaries in an E.E.C. Member country by an enterprise situated in another Member country or in a third country. Acquisitions amounted to only 19 per cent in 1966, 18 per cent in 1970 and 17 per cent in
1971, the majority of international operations being the direct creation of subsidiaries by individual enterprises (58 per cent in 1966,
64 per cent in 1970 and 65 per cent in 1971). These figures suggest
that cross-frontier amalgamations are less favoured in E.E.C. Member
countries than the creation of individual or joint subsidiaries.

129.    Although available statistics are few and very imperfect it
would seem reasonable to conclude that in several OECD Member countries
there has been a significant number of international mergers. It is
important to consider the implications of this for government competition policy and to consider briefly the reasons why firms may prefer
to merge with or acquire a firm in another country rather than establish new facilities by direct investment.

## The Competitive Consequences of Foreign Investment

130.    In analysing the competitive consequences of a foreign acquisition, a distinction should be made between a very small or "foothold"
acquisition, which probably should be treated as if it were new direct
entry, and the acquisition of a leading firm or one with a substantial
market share which is the type of foreign acquisition with which most
of the discussion in this chapter is concerned.

---

1) Second report on competition policy, Commission of the European
   Communities, Brussels-Luxembourg, April 1973, p. 143.

131.    The discussions above on the motives for direct foreign investment, and the directions it will take, have stressed present economic
evidence that a substantial part of it will flow from and into industries  which are more likely to be highly concentrated than less so.
The relationships between concentration and economic performance have
been reported on earlier, in Chapter I, and while their general vali-
dity is not put into question by foreign direct investment, there may
be some additional factors which need to be taken into account. First,
the theoretical analysis (also supported by empirical evidence) suggests that such investment will be made by firms which, when compared
to local manufacturers, may have assets which result in their being
both more efficient and profitable. This greater efficiency enables
them to surmount the barriers to entry which also face a potential
local entrant to an industry. The barriers arising through economies
of scale, product differentiation and absolute levels of capital
requirements  are not those which deter the foreign investor, generally speaking. On the contrary, some of his strength derives from them.
On the other hand, as compared with the potential local entrant, he
does face an information barrier because of lack of local knowledge;
and also barriers because there may be higher risks associated with
foreign, rather than local, investment - even if these are only exchange rate fluctuations.

132.    The discussion, so far, has been in terms of the possible greater efficiency of the multinational corporation, which enables it to
surmount the entry barriers associated with a foreign country. The
efficiencies of the corporation may derive from its size in its home
market, which permit it to enjoy all the available economies of scale;
and while this is likely to be true in large measure, because the
major proportion of foreign investment is made by large firms, there
are also possible economies which may arise out of the multinational
character of the corporation. It appears that by phasing investment
decisions between different production centres multi-plant firms may
enjoy significant cost saving and scale economy - enhancing advantages
in expanding their capacity to meet growing demands. Evidence and
analysis in a forthcoming book by Scherer, Beckenstein, Kaufer and
Murphy (1) indicate that co-ordinated investment phasing may result
in a lower average level of excess capacity, and permit the more effective exploitation of investment scale economies. These may result
in savings of up to 20 per cent of the total discounted value of the
capital plus operating costs. In addition to the possible gains which
might arise from optimal investment phasing over different national
locations, the authors show that in some circumstances there may be

---

1) Scherer, Beckenstein, Kaufer and Murphy : "The Economics of Multi-
   Plant Operation - An International Comparisons Analysis".

substantial economies to be derived from increasing their degree of plant specialisation. In relatively small national markets protected by high tariff barriers the degree of plant specialisation is likely to be small, but as national barriers disappear and tariffs become lower the multi-plant firm is more readily able to concentrate production in specialist plants and they obtain the benefits of considerably larger production runs. Thus, it appears that in certain circumstances the multinational corporation may be able to obtain additional economies which are not readily available to the purely national, generally less specialised firms. However, these economies are important only when the purely national firms are unable or unwilling to trade with each other, so as either to permit more optimal investment phasing or greater specialisation. If these possibilities exist, then the particular efficiency gains may confer no relative advantage to the multi-national corporation. They may, of course, be never realised. If the multinational corporation spreads its operations by transnational mergers, and if it is unable to integrate the acquired firms quickly and effectively into an international network, then the additional efficiencies may never be obtained. As it is possible that many multinational corporations may be unwilling to interfere to any great extent in the operation of national subsidiaries, particularly in the early years after acquisition, it may be that these economies remain as a potential gain rather than become an actual one from international mergers. The Committee finds this evidence and analysis persuasive.

133.    The extent of the balance of advantage deriving from being a foreign entrant, as compared to a national entrant, will, of course, play some part in the decision on how entry is to be made. It may be by the establishment of new productive facilities, by joint ventures or by merger, and will also depend upon the relative prices which the foreign entrant will have to pay for productive resources. In that he may buy these in more than one market he has a corresponding advantage over the local supplier; but as between buying an existing firm or establishing a new one, the influence of the additional information requirement and risks attached to foreign investment may be more important than relative factor prices.

134.    The second factor which needs to be considered is that, because the foreign investor does not have established behaviour patterns in the local market, he may be less likely to accept the joint profit objectives which may have been established by the existing oligopolistic  structures.

135.    If a foreign investor is more efficient and not committed to national oligopoly group objectives his entry is likely to disturb the existing conditions of competition and, at least for some time, this may lead to an intentisification of rivalry, resulting in overall

improved economic performance. This may be particularly so where entry
is made by a new establishment into a concentrated industry, because
the new entrant will have to increase the intensity of competition in
order to grow to the minimum size necessary to attain the profit objectives which stem from the possession of the special asset. During this
period of growth, overall performance is likely, therefore, to be improved.

136.　However, even if the foreign investor enters an industry by merger, and hence does not alter the existing degree of concentration, different behaviour patterns can result in pro-competitive consequences
- at least during the period when the foreign investor is becoming
accustomed to the new environment. To the extent that the purpose of
investing is to take advantage of the higher efficiency stemming from
the special asset it would follow that the investor would not simply
have acquired a local firm for its existing rate of return. The attempt
to improve on this, whether by improved products, productive methods
or sales promotion techniques, is likely to have competitive consequences for all the other firms in the market. These effects must be
balanced against the elimination of the actual (through exports) and
potential competition of the foreign investor which existed prior to
the entry by the merger.

137.　This analysis of the possible consequences of direct inward
investment has been principally concerned with an extension of horizontal activities, and it has been suggested that foreign direct investment can - at least in the initial stages - bring benefits from increased competition. However, it should also be stressed that, because such
investment generally flows from a concentrated industry in one country
into a concentrated industry in another, the overall effect is to increase the degree of concentration in world production and trade; and
there may be substantial disadvantages which stem from this which have
to be offset against what might be the competitive gains from new entry
in a particular industry in a particular country. It follows, therefore,
that no general presumption arises for or against international investment by merger; the costs and benefits are specific to an industry at a
a given time and within the given country or trade group, and each case
must be judged on its merits.

Application of Restrictive Business Practices Legislation to International Mergers

138.　Chapter II has already noted that only 5 Member countries (1)
- Canada, Germany, Japan, the United Kingdom and the United States -

--------------------

1) In addition, a bill to control mergers has recently been introduced
   in Australia whilst in Ireland and the Netherlands mergers legislation is at present under consideration.

have specific systems of merger control within the context of their competition laws. To this must be added the rules of the Rome and Paris Treaties establishing the European Communities which also contain provisions permitting action to be taken against mergers. It is therefore evident that this Section only refers to these 5 Member countries and to the European Communities.

139.    Apart from the specific legislative provisions designed to control mergers in these 5 countries, it should be noted that most Member countries possess foreign exchange control laws or regulations to permit them to assess the balance-of-payments capital account effects of takeovers of domestic by foreign firms or foreign by domestic firms. Moreover, several countries also have legislation designed to protect the national public interest in maintaining certain key sectors of the economy under domestic ownership by preventing or restricting foreign investment in these sectors. In Australia, the Companies (Foreign Takeovers) Act 1972-73 provides for examination of foreign takeover proposals and for the prevention of such takeovers found to be contrary to the national interest. Finally, Governments have other kinds of discretionary powers derived from regional or tax policies which enable them to exercise control over merger and acquisition operations even when no antitrust-policy type of control exists. These policies will not, however, be discussed in detail since they lie outside the scope of a report considering mergers purely from the competition policy viewpoint. They should however not be forgotten as they may well include competition policy-like provisions. For example, in Spain under the Tax Reform Act of 1957, the Ministry of Finance may grant tax concessions to facilitate mergers subject to certain conditions, one of which is that the merger should result in no monopolistic activities. Furthermore, no doubt because of the wider scope of the public interest criterion for assessing mergers, the United Kingdom Monopolies and Mergers Commission has attached special attention in several reports (1) to the monetary and trade effects on the balance of payments of national and (in one case) international mergers which would doubtless fall under other legislation in other countries.

140.    In Canada, no action has been taken pursuant to Section 33 of the Combines Investigation Act against a merger involving a foreign and a Canadian company. In fact only 6 proceedings have been instituted by the Department of Justice under this provision against mergers between Canadian companies only. Four were unsuccessful, one resulted in a plea of guilty and one is still in progress. The penal character of

---

1) See, for example, the reports on the mergers between B.M.C. Limited and Pressed Steel Company Limited (1966), Thorn Electrical Industries and Radio Rentals Limited (1968) and the Rank Organisation Limited and the De La Rue Company Limited (1968).

Section 33 would appear to be responsible for difficulty in bringing successful actions against national and international mergers. On 12th December, 1973, the Foreign Investment Review Act was enacted. A procedure is established for notification of plans by persons other than Canadians to acquire Canadian business enterprises over a specified size or to establish any new business in Canada. Such proposals are to be allowed only if they are likely to be of significant benefit to Canada. A Foreign Investment Review Agency is provided for to assist a Minister to be designated by the Governor in Council, who is to make the assessments and to make recommendations to the Governor in Council. If no action is taken by the Minister within sixty days after notification, the proposal will be deemed to have been allowed. Guidelines for assessment of proposals are provided in section 2 (2) of the Act, which is as follows :

"(2) In assessing, for the purposes of this Act, whether any acquisition of control of a Canadian business enterprise or the establishment of any new business in Canada is or is likely to be of significant benefit to Canada, the factors to be taken into account are as follows :

a) the effect of the acquisition or establishment on the level and nature of economic activity in Canada, including, without limiting the generality of the foregoing, the effect on employment, on resource processing, on the utilisation of parts, components and services produced in Canada, and on exports from Canada;

b) the degree and significance of participation by Canadians in the business enterprise or new business and in any industry or industries in Canada of which the business enterprise or new business forms or would form a part;

c) the effect of the acquisition or establishment on productivity, industrial efficiency, technological development, product innovation and product variety in Canada;

d) the effect of the acquisition or establishment on competition within any industry or industries in Canada; and

e) the compatibility of the acquisition or establishment with national industrial and economic policies, taking into consideration industrial and economic policy objectives enunciated by the government or legislature of any province likely to be significantly affected by the acquisition or establishment."

The part of the Act relating to acquisitions of Canadian enterprises came its effect on 9th April, 1974.

141. In Germany, one action against a merger involving a foreign enterprise has to be mentioned which took place since the adoption of the amendment to the Act Against Restraints of Competition in 1973.

The German enterprise AEG-Telefunken AG planned to acquire 25.01 per cent of the share capital of the Italian producer of electrical household appliances A. Zanussi S.p.A. AEG-Telefunken was submitted a note by the Federal Cartel Office that it might expect a prohibition of the acquisition if it should be effected. It was held (1) that the German merger regulations can be used as Zanussi sells great quantities of its electrical appliances in Germany, its best customer being besides AEG-Telefunken the mail-order house Quelle; (2) that, in regard to different sorts of appliances, the common market share of both enterprises fell within the market share presumptions of the newly amended Section 22 of the Act and (3) that the whole industry showed an already relatively high concentration ratio. AEG-Telefunken then withdrew its notification and acquired only 20 per cent of Zanussi's capital which was accepted by the Federal Cartel Office.

142.    In Japan, no action against a merger or an acquisition involving a foreign enterprise has been taken pursuant to provisions in the Anti-Monopoly Act which prohibits mergers or acquisitions where they may substantially restrain competition in any particular field of trade or where unfair business practices are employed.

143.    In the United Kingdom, only in one report of the Monopolies Commission was the issue directly one of an international merger (1) and here the Commission concluded that there was "no reason why either of the proposed mergers should produce any immediately substantial effect upon the trade in dental goods in the United Kingdom". Some concern was expressed about the effects on overseas trade of a merger between D.S. Company (the United States firm) and A.D. Company, namely that D.S. Company might transfer production of dental goods from the United Kingdom to, for example, the Common Market. The Commission, however, on balance considered this risk to be small (2).

144.    The United States is the only country which in recent years actively applied its legislation to international mergers, primarily under Section 7 of the Clayton Act. Some of these cases have involved foreign companies which have acquired United States companies or their assets. In a 1967 case, the Department of Justice brought an action against a joint venture involving a German company - the Mobay case(3). Mobay was established in 1954 by Monsanto and Bayer, and as a result Monsanto withdrew from producing and selling a certain chemical in the United States and Bayer exported only to Mobay, which acquired 50 per

---

1) The Dental Manufacturing Company Limited, or the Dentists Supply Company of New York and the Amalgamated Dental Company Limited. A report on the proposed mergers (HMSO, 1966).

2) But see note of dissent by one Member of the Commission, Mr. W.E. Jones, idem, p. 45.

3) U.S. v. Monsanto Company, Farbenfabriken Bayer AG and Mobay Chemical Company, CCH Trade Cases 1967, par. 72,001.

cent of the United States market for that product. In a consent settlement of the case Monsanto sold its interest in Mobay to Bayer.

145. Another case concerned Alcan, the United States subsidiary of the Canadian firm Aluminium Limited (1), which was required by a consent decree to divest itself of the assets it had acquired from National Distillers and Chemical Corporation. However, pursuant to the decree, Alcan was relieved of this obligation after it had made a bona fide attempt to find an eligible buyer.

146. In the Atlantic Richfield case (2) involving the proposed merger of two large United States oil companies, Atlantic Richfield proposed to sell off Sinclair's marketing assets in the North-Eastern United States to British Petroleum Limited. The Department of Justice did not object and the court permitted this sale since it would substitute "a new and viable competitor for Sinclair in the North-East".

147. Subsequently, British Petroleum Limited was involved in another merger case involving the Standard Oil Company of Ohio (Sohio) (3). The Department of Justice objected to the merger on the grounds that British Petroleum Limited was a potential entrant into Ohio, Sohio's primary market and the merger would foreclose an independent entry into that market. The case was settled by a consent decree under which the merger was allowed to proceed provided that Sohio divested itself, by sale or exchange for stations in other parts of the country, of stations handling a total of 400 million gallons of petrol per year in the Ohio market.

148. These and other cases indicate that the Department of Justice will challenge acquisitions when a major foreign firm, an actual or potential competitor in the United States market, merges or enters into a joint venture with a major United States firm in a concentrated United States market and the effect is to foreclose independent entry or expansion of the foreign firm. It has been emphasized that the United States welcomes the entry of foreign firms into the United States market independently or by a foothold acquisition that is, acquiring a smaller United States company.

149. Also, the United States has applied its legislation to mergers abroad which have or are likely to have a substantial adverse effect on American commerce. This has invariably involved acquisitions of foreign companies by United States companies, although in one case (4)

---

1) U.S. v. Aluminium Limited, Alcan Aluminium Corporation and National Distillers and Chemical Corporation (DC NJ 1968) CCH Trade Cases 1968, par. 72,631.

2) U.S. v. Atlantic Richfield Company and Sinclair Oil Corporation (SDNY 1969), CCH Trade Cases 1969, par. 72,715.

3) U.S. v. Standard Oil Company (Ohio) et al (DC Ohio 1969).

4) U.S. v. Ciba Corporation et al /̄70 Civ 3078 (SDNY)7.

Section 7 of the Clayton Act was applied in the United States to certain aspects of a merger between two non-American companies each of which had an American subsidiary.

150.    The first case concerned the American brewery Jos. Schlitz which acquired a Canadian company which itself owned a brewery in the United States (1). The court held that the large established Canadian breweries represented the most probable sources of potential competition in the United States.

151.    Another case concerned the acquisition of Braun, a German company, by Gillette on the chief ground that the intended merger would eliminate potential domestic competition since Braun was a potential entrant to the United States market and that Gillette might potentially enter the United States electric shaver market. The case has not yet been settled.

152.    Finally, in the Ciba Corporation et al. case, the Department of Justice attacked a merger between two Swiss companies Ciba and Geigy alleging that the merger would substantially lessen competition in the United States between their wholly-owned subsidiaries in the manufacture and sale of dye-stuffs, certain drugs and herbicides. The merger was allowed pursuant to a settlement requiring the sale of certain assets of the American subsidiaries to restore competition lost by the merger.

153.    In the European Coal and Steel Community, special provisions exist for the High Authority - now the Commission - to control intra-Community mergers in the coal and steel sectors. All direct and indirect concentrations in the Community except insignificant ones which are expressly exempted by Decision 25-67 of 22nd June, 1967, must receive prior authorisation, as mentioned in Chapter II. Pursuant to Article 66 of the Paris Treaty, the High Authority also adopted a decision in 1954 (2) requiring firms located outside the E.C.S.C. to notify the High Authority if they acquire more than 10 per cent of the equity of an E.C.S.C. enterprise amounting to more than 100,000 units of account. However, none of the authorisations granted or refusals have involved firms based outside the E.C.S.C. so that it is not possible to determine the scope of this provision.

154.    Under the Treaty establishing the European Economic Community the Commission has recently applied for the first time Article 86 to a merger involving the Belgian subsidiary of a United States firm (3).

---

1) U.S. v. Jos. Schlitz Brewing Company, 253 F Supp. 129 (1966) aff'd per curiam, 385 U.S. 37 (1966).

2) Decision 26-54 of 6th May, 1954.

3) Commission Decision of 9th December, 1971 - Continental Can Company (Official Journal of the European Communties, L7 of 8th January, 1972).

The case is of special interest therefore, not only because it is the first time the Commission has attempted to apply Article 86 to a concentration but because the acquisition in question involved a parent company located outside the Common Market, albeit operating through its Belgian subsidiary. Article 86 prohibits the abuse of a dominant position in the Common Market or in any substantial part thereof. Already in its 1965 Memorandum to the Governments of Member States on Concentration of Enterprises in the Common Market (1), the Commission took the view that a merger of an enterprise accupying a dominant position with another enterprise, which had the effect of eliminating competition that would continue to exist on the market by creating a monopolistic situation, could constitute an abuse within the meaning of this Article.

155.    In this case the Commission considered that Continental Can by acquiring through its Belgian subsidiary, Europemballage Corporation SA, the Dutch company Thomassen and Driyver-Verblifa NV after already controlling the largest German company in the light metal container industry, Schmalbach-Lubeca-Werke AG, had exploited abusively the dominant position it held in a substantial part of the Common Market (defined as North-West Europe)  in that competition was in practice eliminated in this area for the products in question and that, in particular, this concentration had an unfavourable effect on competition by restricting excessively the choice of consumers of certain types of container. Continental Can was given until 1st July, 1972, to submit proposals to the Commission to terminate its infringement of Article 86.

156.    Continental Can took the case to the Court of Justice of the European Communities. In its judgment of 21st February, 1973, the Court quashed the decision of the Commission on the grounds that the latter had not sufficiently defined the market in question. However, the Court confirmed the Commission's interpretation of Article 86 as to the applicability of this Article to certain concentrations. It decided that there was an abuse falling under Article 86 when "an enterprise in a dominant position strengthened this position to the point where the degree of domination thus achieved hampered competition to an appreciable extent, i.e. would leave only enterprises depending, in their action, on the dominant enterprise".

157.    This brief account of cases of international mergers demonstrates that, up to the present, merger control provisions have been applied only in Germany, the United States, the United Kingdom and the European Communities to international mergers. It should also be added that the number of cases investigated or brought before the court is still

---

1) Memorandum of 1st December, 1965.

limited. However, the number of cases dealt with is not in itself significant, for the very existence of a control of international mergers plays a part in preventing anti-competitive international mergers.

## General Conclusions

158.    The effects upon competition of international mergers are analytically similar to those of domestic mergers, although they sometimes present special problems of evaluation at the national level. On the one hand, unlike purely domestic horizontal mergers, international mergers in some circumstances do not have any adverse effect on concentration at the national level, and they can be a means of introducing vigorous new competition, particularly where the company acquired is a small "foothold" company. It is also possible, of course, that the merger may not improve a non-competitive situation, and may even worsen it if the acquired firm has a large market share. The financial and other resources of the acquiring company can then be used to exploit and increase the already large market share of the acquired company. In addition, a merger which has no effect upon concentration in the countries directly involved may nevertheless increase it at the world level or in third countries. Moreover, an international merger may in some cases lead to restrictions on the freedom of the acquired company to compete in certain product lines or export markets. Also, national control over international mergers sometimes presents jurisdictional and informational problems not encountered in purely domestic mergers. Finally, there is the point that excess profits resulting from international mergers are different to an important degree from excess profits resulting from national mergers, in that the latter involve a domestic redistribution of income whereas the former involve a transfer of income between countries.

159.    These considerations seem to point to the conclusion that, at the present time, viewed from the standpoint of their competitive effects, international mergers should, like national mergers, be treated on their respective merits, that is whether they are likely to increase competition in production, distribution and research and therefore the competitiveness of a country's economy or whether, on the other hand, they may create undue concentrations of economic power or otherwise injure competition. This judgement can only be made on a case-by-case basis.

160.    There are sufficient indications in some Member countries of a continuing trend towards increased aggregate concentration to suggest the need for the adoption or strengthening of control of both national and international mergers. Possible conflicts between Member countries in the field of international mergers arising out of divergent national merger policies could be reduced if Member countries work towards

similar standards and approaches for assessing and dealing with mergers. Moreover, another problem not exclusive to international mergers but requiring an international solution is the extra-territorial application or effect of competition policies. Although the cases mentioned in this report do not lend support to the view that there are frequent conflicts between Member countries in the field of international mergers, in the event that such extra-territorial application or effect possibly creates difficulties, a solution might be achieved under the 1967 OECD Council Recommendation concerning co-operation between Member countries on restrictive business practices affecting international trade /C̄(67)53(Final)7 or under the 1973 OECD Council Recommendation concerning a consultation and conciliation procedure on restrictive business practices affecting international trade /C̄(73) 99 (Final7 or perhaps through creation of some sort of new international anti-trust co-ordination arrangement.

Chapter IV

## CONCLUSIONS, POLICY OPTIONS AND SUGGESTIONS FOR FUTURE ACTION

### Introduction

161.   It should be noted at the beginning of this concluding chapter
that there is not necessarily any single policy towards mergers which
must be recommended to Governments considering the introduction or
amendment of legislation dealing with mergers. The wide differences
in economic, social and legal environments between countries have to
be recognised. While it can be agreed that some mergers have injurious
economic, social and possibly political effects, the relative importance of merger as a means of corporate growth differs as between countries and hence it would be expected that the extent and overall consequences as regards the impairment of economic performance would also
differ. In addition, there are frequently many ways of offsetting or
compensating for deficient economic performance, and hence remedies
would also be expected to differ as between countries. Each particular
merger must therefore be studied for its effects.

162.   However, while it is correct to stress that diversity of national environments does not lead to any unique conclusions about merger
control, it must also be stressed that there are major economic forces
at work which do highlight the need for most countries with developed
economies to recognise that the question of mergers and merger control
does require consideration. Three major elements of the economic environment which raise the question of mergers can be distinguished.
First, as the data in Chapter I show, overall concentration is, and has
increased substantially, in the United States of America, Germany and
the United Kingdom. This is also true in other Member States of the
European Communities. While comparable data are not available from
other countries, so that the extent and development of overall concentration cannot be measured, there seems little reason to doubt that it
is a process which is taking place in all countries. These forces,
which lead to a differential growth rate for the larger firms and
operate in all market economies, do not, of course, necessarily do so
at the same intensity.

163.   While the part played by merger in increasing concentration will
also differ as between countries, both in its importance relative to

the internal growth of firms and to other economic forces which might lead to de-concentration, the governmental or non-governmental encouragements to merge have very probably led to an increased rate of merger in many countries (1).

164. The second major influence on the rate of growth of firms is the increasing integration of national markets, because of the high and sustained rate of growth of international trade. Reduced tariff and non-tariff barriers and other trade liberalising measures are resulting in national markets becoming more and more integrated with each other. The consequence of this is that imports generally have become a more important factor in the competitive situation, and the opportunities for exports have been another major influence affecting the growth of firms.

165. The third factor is closely related to the first and second, and is the growing importance of the multinational firm in national and international trade. As international trade increases so do the opportunities for international investment and indeed they are closely related to each other in a causal way. This suggests that national competitive conditions are likely to be affected by the entry of multinational firms as well as by imports. In addition, while international investment may be a substitute for international trade to some degree, it appears that an increasing proportion of world trade is being conducted by multinational firms. As these tend to be large the long-run trend may be towards an increasing degree of concentration in international trade.

166. A related factor influencing the development of conglomerate mergers has probably been the acceleration in the rate of development of technology which enhances the attraction of the security derived from diversification.

167. These 4 major economic influences are having important repercussions on the structure of national economies. The financial and technological forces which tend to promote the growth of the larger firms are reinforced by the growth of world trade - by removing one barrier, the absolute size of market. To counterbalance these tendencies, increasing imports and the growth of the multinational corporations have probably increased the intensity of competition in national and inter-

---

1) In the United Kingdom, for example, the Industrial Reorganisation Corporation was established in 1966 and operated until 1971 as a Government Agency to bring about the re-structuring of certain industries where it was thought that the existing operation of market forces was preventing the most efficient types of industrial structures from emerging. It is estimated that the IRC played an important part in 30 major mergers, as well as actively encouraging and supporting about 100 others. It is also thought that the majority of these resulted in an increased industrial concentration.

national markets by providing opportunities for new firms and new products to be established. While it is difficult, in the absence of detailed studies, to be certain about the overall direction and strength of these forces it would appear to be reasonable to suppose that the net result is likely to be an increasing degree of concentration in national and international markets. This raises the policy questions of the public control over this phenomenon.

## The policy issues

168.    In considering the question of increasing concentration and its effects, the principal economic issues are :
   a) the existing levels of overall and market concentration and their rates of growth;
   b) The relative importance of merger, as distinct form internal growth of firms, as the cause of increasing concentration;
   c) The identification, measurement and balance of the beneficial and detrimental effects of merger;
   d) The principles determining the type of machinery which may be used to operate merger control.

## The level and growth of concentration

169.    In Chapter I a distinction was made between overall concentration and market concentration. The former describes the degree of ownership and control over certain economic resources across a national economy, while the latter describes the degree of ownership and control within one industry. A prior condition for considering the level and growth of concentration is that it should be adequately measured and described. This may be done, for example, in terms of capital, profits, sales or employment and, for policy purposes, any single one of these could be adequate as an indicator of trends' levels.

170.    The concern about increasing overall and market concentration arises among other reasons because of the effects which it may have on economic structure and performance and thereby on the attainment of national economic objectives. Sufficient evidence is available to show that deficient economic performance often results directly from situations of high concentration, and these deficiencies may take the form of very high prices and profits or, alternatively, high costs including excessive product differentiation and selling expenditures, low technical efficiency, a lack of technical aggressiveness and poor international competitiveness. Because of the relative importance in

national economies of imports, countervailing buying power, Government
controls and other economic factors which offset or restrain the exercise of market power, it is not possible to indicate with any degree
of generality what levels of concentration do produce these detrimental
effects. However, while the question of what may be regarded as high
concentration is essentially a matter for national decision, what can
hardly be disputed is that merger appears to be a major cause of it
and may therefore be a potential major source of economic detriment.
Also, the evidence about the growth of concentration strongly suggests
that the forces which make for de-concentration have been considerably
outweighed by those which lead to increasing concentration; and this
appears to be an almost inevitable process. Thus the rate at which
concentration increases is as of much concern as the absolute levels.

## The Relative Importance of Merger and Internal Growth

171.    While the measurement of concentration is generally considered
to be essential it is, nevertheless, only a starting point for the
consideration of the policy issues. It was suggested above that there
may be very strong economic forces which are tending to favour the
growth of larger firms relative to the smaller, so that the process
of increasing economic concentration may frequently accompany such
growth in size. However, a very real distinction must be made between
the internal growth which can occur when some firms recognise and adapt
themselves more efficiently to meet changing consumer demands at lower
real costs, and external growth by merger which may merely result in
the growth of the firm with no corresponding improvements for consumers
or in the lowering of real costs. The internal growth of the firm,
when it derives from lower costs and/or the more efficient meeting of
consumer demands, will, at least during the growth stage, result in
more competitive markets, and this will bring real economic benefits
to society. External growth may also bring such benefits, but on the
other hand, it may only result in an increase in market power with
detrimental consequences for economic performance, as well as adverse
social and political consequences.

172.    One qualification may, however, be necessary to this statement.
If a particular merger is likely to produce significant gains in terms
of efficiency, the speed with which these are realised compared with
internal growth may be a factor to be weighed against the immediate
market power consequences of the merger. A merger which results in the
much earlier achievement of efficiency gains than by internal growth
may be socially preferred. It is however worthwhile to consider whether
many efficiencies might not also be achieved by measures short of merger or by mergers which do not raise issues of competition policy.

## The Balance of Benefits and Detriments from Merger

173.    In the chapter which examined the economic effects of mergers a distinction was made between conglomerate or diversified mergers which increased overall concentration and horizontal or vertical mergers which also increased market concentration. The effects of these 2 types may be different and could lead to different policy options.

174.    One of the issues in the horizontal and vertical merger case is the trade-off between potential increased efficiency and the increased market power providing the potential for anti-competitive abuses. Potential increases in efficiency should be understood in a wide sense subject to a realistic estimate whether they are likely to be realised and whether they can only be realised by a merger of this type. They would include the opportunity to take advantage of economies of scale in production, sales, management, finance and research and development, multi-plant workings and any other efficiencies which may be obtained. In addition, the effects of the merger on growth prospects and, in particular, foreign trade may be important. To counterbalance this there is the danger that a higher degree of concentration, and hence market power, may lead to some kind of monopolistic or oligopolistic abuse. This may take the form of higher than normal profits, thus reducing overall economic welfare and perhaps adversely affecting the distribution of income. Alternatively, the economic performance of merged firms may deteriorate absolutely, also causing a reduction in economic welfare. One inevitable adverse result of every horizontal merger,  except perhaps one with a failing company, is that it eliminates one competitor and reduces the independent factors operating in the market. The dynamic effects on industry structure must also be considered in this context, if the merger triggers off other defensive groupings amongst firms which do not result in increased efficiency. Each horizontal or vertical merger should therefore be examined in the light of its particular effects, subject, of course, to judicial, administrative or legislative rules based on accumulated experience for policy analysis.

175.    The issues arising from the conglomerate or diversified merger are, to some extent, different as, by definition, there is not an increase in concentration in individual markets. However, absolute size by itself may have 2 types of economic disadvantage : it may result in an overall decline in performance if the firm exceeds the size at which it can be efficiently operated with given techniques of production and management and it may also give the firm the power to indulge in certain types of market behaviour, which may have damaging consequences for competition. Size may bring increased overall financial power of a kind which permits cross-subsidisation in the markets in which the firm operates, reciprocal dealings with other

large and conglomerate firms, retrenchment of the dominant position of the acquired firm and it may also permit the firm to alter market structures by the relatively easy acquisition of potential competitors. On the other hand, the conglomerate or diversified merger may be a legitimate form of firm growth if it is based on existing specialities, skills and efficiencies which may be transferred to other markets at little or no real economic cost, or if it facilitates the provision of capital for modernisation. In these cases the entry of the firm into a new market may disturb existing structures and behaviour patterns in such a way that the intensity or forms of competition change so as to increase economic welfare. It would appear therefore that any particular conglomerate needs to be studied for its effects in individual markets before any overall judgement can be made.

176.    The discussion has been about mergers which have beneficial or detrimental economic effects and, while it is true that all mergers have some of these, it must be recognised that many mergers which take place are small and insignificant in terms of the economic welfare of a nation. There are also strong economic forces which lead to the birth and death of firms and, as new entrants to an industry provide the seed-bed for new products and perhaps greater competition, it is important that there should be as few impediments as possible to their growth. In the growth process many small - and medium-sized firms may reach a stage when additional financial, managerial or other resources are needed, and merger may be an economically and socially acceptable method of making these available. Also, expectation of the ability to sell a successful small business may in itself be an incentive to entry. It would follow, therefore, that there will be many mergers which, because of their size and economic impact, are not likely to be the concern of public policy which deals with the diminution of competition. It is even possible that many of these mergers will further competitive ends. At what size and what kinds of mergers the dividing line is drawn is a matter which can only be decided in the light of the conditions within each country.

## The Principles and Machinery of Merger control

177.    Although there are, in practice, substantial common elements in the systems of merger control which have been described earlier, it is possible to see that there are 2 different, though related, approaches to problems of enhanced market power. The first places stress on the absolute value of competition as a regulator of economic activity and is seen, for example, in the United States where the possible advantages of a merger cannot be pleaded to offset the disadvantages which would result from increased concentration. The second approach is, as in the United Kingdom, where the promotion and maintenance of effective

competition is one of a number of other desirable objectives : for example, employment, the distribution of industry and the balance-of-payments. However, as was stressed earlier, this report is not concerned with making judgements about the respective merits of the different approaches to merger control which have been adopted.

178.    One common feature to the systems which exist is the recognition of the importance of reducing uncertainty about the acceptability of an actual or proposed merger. This finds expression in 3 ways :

a) In prescribed time periods within which authorities must indicate their intentions and/or judgements;

b) In the establishment of limits below which mergers are not subject to control;

c) In more or less specific indications of the considerations which are taken into account in the particular cases which are subject to control.

179.    Although some countries have predominantly either a pre- or post-notification system of control, it has been found, in practice, that pre-notification, whether formal or informal, has been an extremely valuable method of reducing the uncertainty as to what the ultimate decision would be. For example, in Canada the Director of Investigation and Research has prepared a list of criteria by which possible illegality may be tested, and in the United Kingdom the Secretary of State for Prices and Consumer Protection will decide whether a particular merger should be referred to the Monopolies and Mergers Commission, which is the body with responsibility for deciding whether the actual or proposed merger is against the public interest.

180.    The question of the lower limit of merger control is essentially one to be settled within a given national context, taking into account the existing level of concentration, its rate of growth, its composition and the existence of countervailing power whether private or Governmental. What does appear to be clear from differing national experiences and approaches to problems of market domination, is that many of the mergers which take place do not raise, in any practical or measurable sense, serious questions of reduction of competition or detriment to the general interest; so whatever the system of control it is usually only concerned with relatively few mergers which do raise these questions. It may be that no precise guidelines can be laid down whichwould be of general applicability; some nations state limits in terms of market share, and others in terms of market share and size of enterprises, measured for example by assets or turnover.

181.    The remaining question of the considerations which will be taken into account in a particular merger present the most difficulty in providing an answer. There may be no ideal solution to the problems raised by increased concentration which come about by merger, and those which

have been attempted have had only limited success in halting the major merger movements which have taken place. Nevertheless the lack of an ideal and generally applicable solution is not an argument for not attempting to regulate and reduce the social costs which do often flow from a limited number of mergers which confer only private advantage through enhanced market power.

## International Mergers

182.    The data presented in the chapter on international mergers show, for those countries with records, that these may be a major component of all merger activity and therefore they cannot be ignored on the grounds of infrequent occurrence. International mergers are a form of direct inward investment, and as such raise basically similar problems of efficiency and competition as do domestic mergers. There is evidence to suggest that this type of merger may result from the desire to exploit some differential advantage, whether it be efficiency or product differentiation; and as a consequence their predominant form is horizontal rather than vertical or diversified. This may not, of course, raise concentration levels in host countries but it does so when the world market for the product is considered, and this may have long-term detrimental consequences. In the short-term, on the other hand, it is suggested that international mergers based on differential efficiency may result in increased competition in host country markets because the foreign entrant would wish to exploit this advantage; and will also not have absorbed any prevailing non-competitive behaviour patterns. For these reasons it is not possible to reach any general conclusions about the effect of international mergers; like many domestic mergers they need to be considered as individual cases.

183.    In those countries with merger control systems international mergers have only been rarely considered. Canada and Japan have so far not taken action against mergers between foreign entrants and their own national firms, while in the United Kingdom only one such case was considered and this was found unlikely to operate against the public interest. A few cases have occurred in the United States of America, and these have been judged in terms of their effects on competition, the predominant consideration being foreclosure of markets and restraint of expansion of actual or potential competitors in concentrated industries. A similar consideration arose with the Continental Can case in the European Economic Community. In view of this relative lack of experience it can be tentatively suggested that few international mergers have yet raised problems of enhanced market power, but where they have they have been judged strictly in accordance with competition policy considerations.

184. Although there have only been a relatively small number of international mergers which have appeared to raise questions for competition policy so far, it is likely that the continual growth in international investment and the integration of world markets will lead to many more such cases in the future. The evidence does not suggest that jurisdictional and other problems have yet arisen, but as this may well change in the future with an increased number of international mergers there are good grounds for suggesting that it would be valuable for there to be an international exchange of information and, where necessary, consultations about such mergers.

## Suggestions for Future Action by Member Countries

185. The accelerating trend towards merger together with the already high level of concentration in a number of economic sectors draws attention to the problems of competition which are created by changing market structures and it seems therefore appropriate at the present time to suggest to Member countries which have not yet done so to consider the adoption of an effective system of merger control.

186. The following characteristics might be taken into account :
   i) a procedure for registering mergers, wherever this is felt necessary;
   ii) a system to facilitate obtaining information about occurence of major mergers, such as requiring their prior notification;
   iii) minimum quantitative criteria below which mergers would not be subject to control;
   iv) objective criteria or presumptions for use in evaluating mergers;
   v) reasonable time limits for deciding initially whether to allow or challenge certain mergers.

187. With respect to the application of national laws to mergers and acquisitions involving foreign enterprises and any conflicts which may arise from such an application, Member countries are invited to have recourse to the OECD Council Recommendation of 1967 concerning co-operation between Member countries in the field of restrictive business practices affecting international trade and to the OECD Council Recommendation of 1973 concerning a consultation and conciliation procedure on restrictive business practices affecting international trade.